Panonomics

Clare Devaney

Panonomics

A 4.0 System to Save Us from Ourselves

palgrave
macmillan

Clare Devaney
School of the Built Environment
University of Salford
Salford, UK

ISBN 978-3-030-87508-4 ISBN 978-3-030-87509-1 (eBook)
https://doi.org/10.1007/978-3-030-87509-1

This Palgrave Macmillan imprint is published by the registered company Springer Nature Switzerland AG
The registered company address is: Gewerbestrasse 11, 6330 Cham, Switzerland

Preface

Panonomics is a book about place and time. It is a book of and for the now as a place and time, a book that draws on the lessons of the past and a book that is of and for the future. It is a book that acknowledges the rapid ascension of the concept of 'place' in policymaking, and which explores potential for embracing the richness and diversity of place as a driver for progress. It is a book that recognises the criticality of time, and which proposes that our primary individual and collective mission in life should be the pro-active accumulation of more of it. Written in the midst and latter stages of the COVID-19 pandemic, this book presents panonomics as a response to the increasingly apparent, urgent and critical imperative for a new organisational system; one that is capable of encompassing and embracing holism, universality, complexity, diversity and intersectionality, that can offer fairness, equality and justice, support resistance and resilience in the face of future crises, and which is able to maintain and sustain the human species, other species and our shared planet.

There is considerable irony in my writing a book about time. I am notoriously late, to the extent that good friends have created the concept of 'DevvoTime' in reference to the time that I show up for meetings and engagements. I have an aversion to ticking clocks. I have never owned or worn a watch. While I accept humbly that my lateness must have been frustrating for friends who have stuck with me through the tardiness, it is only as I advance toward middle age that I have become increasingly aware of time, realising that time is the essential metric and the measure of life. Panonomics proposes an organisational model that recognises the centrality and criticality of time, and which is directed toward making more of it.

The COVID-19 pandemic and its lockdowns have both distorted our relationship with time and have created plenty of it for reflection and contemplation. In addition to the rapid consumption of various films, boxsets and streamed television series, my lockdown thoughts have covered space and time, spacetime, the distinction between place and space, and the potential for place as a driver for progress within a new organisational framework. I know that I am by no means alone in imagining what a 'new normal' might look like. Organised through a series of interrogatives (the what, the where, the how, the why, the who and the when), this book explores a range of key concepts including place, time, innovation, growth, care, citizenship, productivity, economics and wellbeing, asserting a new conceptual framework which elevates those key concepts and a series of previously established tripartite models and understandings to a fourth, holistic level of understanding; characterised as 'A Fourth Way'.

Panonomics is a call to arms for a move to a fit for purpose organisational system, and a comprehensive rejection of those structures and institutions which promote inequality and polarisation and which are therefore no longer fit for purpose, including the economic system itself. Too many proposals for radical change have been caught in the anachronisms of orthodox economics and its horsemen of scarcity, profit, growth and productivity, which has resulted in awkward consensus and the rise of uncomfortable compound terms such as 'inclusive growth', 'gross domestic wellbeing' and, latterly, 'community capitalism'. Panonomics builds on the holistic, fourth space principles of 'A Fourth Way' to instead present a framework capable of fluidity and flex in a rapidly changing context and landscape, and which is able, as such, to host new thinking without compromise. Although the book may be of particular interest to thinkers and practitioners working in broad fields of economics and social change, there are universal messages too around equality, sustainability and progress.

The thoughts and arguments presented in this book are well practised thanks to the unfailing ears, love, support and encouragement of my family and friends. My deepest love and thanks to them all and especially to my Mum, my first and lifelong friend and teacher, and to my partner Olie, who has been as kind and generous with his vast intellect and knowledge as he is with everything else. Grateful thanks to Ruth Jenner and Manikandan Murthy at Palgrave Macmillan for their belief in the proposal and the project, their editorial and production expertise and supreme patience. Thanks also to Dr. Claudia Trillo at the University of Salford and to all of our colleagues within the MAPS-LED International Research Partnership.

Though ambitious in both scope and proposals, this concise book is presented as just a drop in an ocean of new thinking, with the hope and intent of causing a few ripples. It is a privilege to be working in this space at a pivotal time of change, and I am blessed to know so many pioneering thinkers and dedicated changemakers, and to count many of them as colleagues and friends. Even in the darkest of times, you help me to believe that we can make a better world.

We can make a better world.

Liverpool, UK
July 2021

Clare Devaney

Contents

CHAPTER 1

Panonomics: 'The What'

Abstract This book presents a vision for a new and holistic organising system—*panonomics*. Etymologically, panonomics takes from the Greek *pan* for 'all' and *nomos* for 'accounts', but unlike its 'economics' (from *oiko* and *nomos*, or 'home accounts') predecessor, it is not just about looking after one's own house, but instead is about looking after everybody's house. Presented as a fitting organisational response to a pandemic, the panonomic framework plots place and time, proposing a comprehensive understanding of 'place' as a foundation for the new organisational system, encompassing a whole spectrum of human creativity, knowledge, skills and life experience and adding a critical dynamism, motility and directionality to drive progress in an onward and upward motion, toward a shared mission. The panonomic model proposes that the organisational framework, and shared mission, should no longer be based on extraction, endless growth and the accumulation of wealth for some and debt for others, but instead prioritise contribution, sustainability and the accumulation of our most precious resource: *time*. While ambitious in both scope and proposals, the book sets out a theoretical context and framework for panonomics and models how it can be applied to current and emerging policy asserting that, through expanding and extending our understandings of key concepts such as place, time and innovation, we can break free from the confines of current and regressive economic structures, systems and institutions to instead advance collectively toward a 'future now'.

C. Devaney, *Panonomics*,
https://doi.org/10.1007/978-3-030-87509-1_1

Keywords Panonomics · A Fourth way · Place · Time · Innovation · Future now

1.1 Introduction: COVID-19: Crisis and Change

The COVID-19 pandemic has brought extreme and unprecedented challenges to a world already crumbling under the pressure of war, famine, climate collapse, stark inequalities and austerity, the killing of George Floyd, the reign (and extended departure, and legacy) of former US President Trump, devastating wildfires in Australia and California, the rise of far-right ideologies and the ever-present spectre of Brexit. The pandemic, the vast and still-growing number of lives that it has cost, its direct and indirect toll on our individual and collective physical and mental health, the extraordinary actions and behaviours it has necessitated, and its disproportionate impacts have combined to devastating effect, thoroughly exposing the limitations of the current economic organisational model. In early 2020, the global stock market faced its worst crash since the 2008 crisis, dropping sharply between February 2020 and April 2020. The World Bank has since reported a global contraction of 5.2% over 2020. To give some indication of scale, the 2008 crisis saw a contraction of just 0.1% (The World Bank 2020).

2021 sees a world adapting to a long-term crisis. 'Lockdowns', social distancing and face masks have been integrated rapidly into daily lives and the social conscious. There is an almost perceptible sense of instability, insecurity and transience, and of not knowing what comes next. Naturally, this circumstance brings with it fear and uncertainty, permitting and giving rise to the whole spectrum of negativity, panic and despair, but what also lives here is *hope*. As Carlota Perez observes, every noted period of industrial discovery and enlightenment throughout history has been immediately preceded by an intense period of crisis—a turning point (Perez 2016). Perez envisages the time immediately ahead of us as the 'sustainable age of technology', a 'Smart Green' golden age (Perez 2016). This forthcoming period is widely referred to as the 'Fourth Industrial Revolution' (Schwab 2016; World Economic Forum 2017) and characterised by Otto Scharmer (2016) as 'Economy 4.0'.

Scharmer describes 4.0 as a shift into what he calls 'ecosystem economics' (Scharmer 2016), characterised not only by a sharply focussed awareness of the global economy as a networked, reciprocal ecosystem but by a deep understanding of the role of the individual as a direct contributor to and within that global ecosystem. Scharmer describes the 4.0 ecosystem as the next level in a sequential evolution of dominant economic schools, having previously travelled through state-centric (1.0), free market (2.0) and socioeconomics (3.0). This shift sits alongside entry into the 'Fourth Industrial Revolution' (World Economic Forum 2017), journeying over four centuries through the first industrial revolution of the 1780s, moving to mass production through steam and electricity in the 1870s, automation in the 1950s and the mass adoption of digital technology through the 1990s and 2000s. (World Economic Forum 2017) Human contribution is critical to the 4.0 economic 'ecosystem' (Scharmer 2016). The World Economic Forum identifies the top three skills required by technology companies in the 4IR as complex problem solving, critical thinking and creativity (World Economic Forum 2016). All three are innately human skills, despite a general understanding of the 'Fourth Industrial Revolution' (4IR) as the coming of a technological age (World Economic Forum 2017).

As we navigate our way into the 4.0 age, there is a growing tension with the paradigm, infrastructure, tools and evaluation mechanisms designed in support of the 'old economics' (Kleibrink et al. 2016). Broadly speaking, this tension is underpinned by an entrenched school of thought which separates the 'economic' and the 'social', and which tends to define 'economic' in purely fiscal terms. In this polarised understanding, the understood economic 'mission' is wealth generation, and the principal measure of success is an accumulation of wealth (Blakely 2019). This is the paradigm of capital, of GDP, of an understanding of human endeavour purely as 'productivity' and of people as generators of product in a labour market. It is the paradigm of economics 2.0, the limitations of which were felt in 3.0, but which are arguably even more acute in our move to 4.0. There is an increasingly apparent need for a new measurement system to support a critical shift from a principally *extractive* economy to a *generative* economy (Kelly, 2013); one in which the objective is not the accumulation of wealth, but which instead focusses on our collective wellbeing and our capacity to meet our most pressing shared challenge: the sustainability of our species and planet.

Demonstrating the need for change, a series of new, alternative systems of governance and better models of economic, spatial and social arrangement have been proposed in recent years, including inclusive growth (RSA 2017), green growth (OECD 2011), degrowth (Jackson 2009; Kallis et al. 2020; Hickel 2020), definancialisation (Blakely 2019), Doughnut Economics (Raworth 2017), mission-oriented economics (Mazzucato 2017 and 2021) and wellbeing economics (Trebeck and Williams 2019; Hoekstra et al. 2020). Internationally, Iceland, New Zealand, Germany and Scotland have led the way in pursuing wellbeing economies, with New Zealand being the first to introduce a 'wellbeing budget' in 2019 and a corresponding dashboard of performance indicators in 2020.

Despite these signs of progress, the capitalist organisational model remains dominant. Its limitations and the structural inequalities present within the free market ideology have been roundly exposed by the market's inability to realise an effective response to the COVID-19 pandemic. A clue as to why lies in the pandemic's prefix. The market's need for imbalance and inequality, for supply and demand, for winners and losers, makes it impotent against something which is *pan-*; all-encompassing, a universal need, and one which requires an all-encompassing, universal response. In the UK, policies have been developed throughout the COVID-19 crisis which have, in effect, created what might be called 'false market' conditions. This includes, for example, the restricted supply of testing services, privatisation of key supply contracts and implementation of a tiered system of localised lockdowns. Thanks to various qualifying criteria, an estimated three million self-employed people across the UK were left without access to the Government's furlough scheme. In December 2020, the UK Government announced that businesspeople involved in trade deals resulting in over fifty jobs or over £100,000 investment in the UK would be exempted from quarantine regulations. Neither of these approaches recognise the universality of the pandemic. The market's impotency has been proven further still by the approach to the rollout of the vaccination, which has seen an unedifying race for patent, questionable contracting of private sector providers and countries with the most need subject to restricted supply. The capitalist model simply cannot offer a holistic solution.

The pandemic has also tested much of the rhetoric behind the concept of an economy which places society in the antonym and in particular the false dichotomy of the economy versus health. It has become abundantly clear that population health and the health of the economy are integral to each other and cannot be separated in this way, even when the thought of at the (too) basic level of protecting the health of an economic workforce.

Simply put, without people, there is no economy. When people stop, the economy stops.

Still, cities and regions across the UK continue to put forward 'bounce back' plans to recover from the impacts of COVID-19 based on the Government's call to 'Build Back Better', many of which feature and are founded on large-scale investment in 'oven ready' capital projects. Not only is this blinkered focus on capital development the very behaviour which saw us hurtling toward the 2008 financial crash, but there is seemingly scant regard in these plans for the impending climate crisis. In many ways, the response is all too human. We have found ourselves reverting to the last time that we felt secure. Little surprise that the rallying call for UK cities is to 'Build Back Better' when nostalgia for the 1990s abounds. Building our way out of a pandemic is accompanied by misty-eyed remembrance of non-stop credit and mortgages on tap, and fond memories of the security of the centre ground 'Third Way' favoured by both the UK Blair government and the US Clinton administration. Both the UK and the US have rejected recent challenges from left-wing socialist leaders. There is perceived safety in the middle.

Building backwards in this way cannot bring progress. Clinging on to notions of growth, productivity, capital wealth and GDP while facing down a dual hit of pandemic and climate collapse is futile. More of the same will just not cut it. Quantitative easing is not enough (despite the UK Government finding £150 billion just prior to the November 2020 lockdown). Throwing money at the situation, even in the guise of a universal basic income, is not enough. Initiatives designed to reform/rethink/reimagine capitalism are not enough. A return to 'Third Way' thinking is not enough.

Economics cannot save us now.

1.2 Panonomics: A New Paradigm for the 4.0 Age

This book presents a new organising paradigm: *panonomics*.

Etymologically, panonomics takes from the Greek pan for 'all' and nomos for 'accounts', but unlike its 'economic' (from oiko and nomos, or 'home accounts') predecessor, it is not just about looking after one's own house, but instead is about looking after everybody's house. In the oikos of Ancient Greece, a term for an extended family (and all of its goods, property and possessions) operating as a single economic unit, the home accounts were traditionally the responsibility of the family's eldest son. In the fluid and feminist panonomic household, there is no such patriarchal lineage. Everybody contributes and is valued equally.

Panonomics—a fitting organisational response to a pandemic—offers an umbrella term within which to unite a broad scope of new economic thinking, freed from the dominance of neoclassical economics, the heavy burden of orthodox economic history and a subsequent dismissal as alternative modelling or, at best, containment as heterodox theory. Gently inspired by panonomics, the approach used in systemic health analytics which integrates multi-dimensional data from across various patient health and molecular biology indicators (such as genomics and proteomics), panonomics offers a similarly integrative platform for the many and various current and emerging 'alternative' economic models. The panonomic framework, for example, allows for macro concepts such as the mission-oriented approach to economics put forward by Mazzucato (2017, 2021) and the grassroots practice of Community Wealth Building (Guinan et al. 2020) to be comfortably embraced within its holism and orientation toward collective progress.

Panonomics is founded on the idea of a 'fourth space', conceived as a successor to 'third space' theory (Soja 1996), and its application as a 'Fourth Way' policy paradigm, conceived as a successor to the favoured 'Third Way' (Giddens 1991) thinking of neoliberalism and the centre ground. In the fourth space, thinking and practice are elevated beyond the two-dimensional confines of polarised binaries, while the compromised consensus of the 'third space' middle ground is also rejected in favour of an all-embracing and holistic systemic model.

Adoption of the new fourth space framework and its policy application as 'A Fourth Way' means that there is no longer a need to operate within the constricts of polarities or to choose for instance between economic and social value, or between health and the economy, nor to seek compromise by awkwardly ascribing economic value to health, because health and social value are recognised as integral to—and of equal standing within—the panonomic model.

1.3 Of Place and Time

The panonomic framework plots place and time as horizontal and vertical axes across the fourth space (Fig. 1.1), proposing a comprehensive understanding of 'place' as the horizontal base for the new organisational

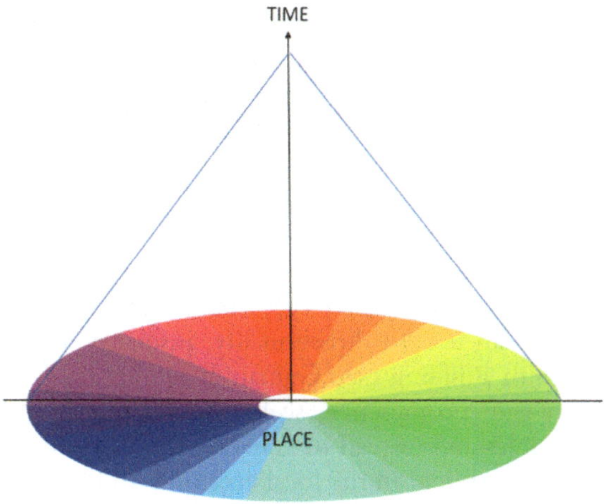

Fig. 1.1 The panonomic framework—Plotting place and time

system which encompasses a whole spectrum of human creativity, knowledge, skills and life experience and adding a critical dynamism, motility and directionality, driving progress as an upward spiral toward a shared mission. The model proposes that our collective priority, and shared mission, should no longer be focussed on building back better to productivity, endless growth and the accumulation of wealth for some and debt for others, but should instead move in a progressive onward and upward trajectory (as the vertical axis of the panonomic model), focussed on collective contribution to human and planetary sustainability goals and the accumulation of our most precious resource: *time*.

The concept of place, which prior to the pandemic had seen a rapid integration into policy, continues to loom large in (primarily urban) development strategy, policy development and practice, sitting alongside the ongoing devolution agenda in the UK, and renewed calls for localism (amplified further by the pandemic and lockdowns). To date, and perhaps related to the speed of its initial ascent and conceptual incompleteness, 'place' has been primarily interpreted either in spatial terms, as a fixed geographic territory, or as a self-contained socio-economic system. The well-practised tenets of place as a set, bordered geography or a set, bordered socio-economy, fit place comfortably within the current and predominantly capital-driven economic paradigm, where the territorial understanding fits neatly with the notion of capital's 'spatial fix' (Harvey 2001) and the socio-economic application of 'place' mimics the defined parameters of the labour market. Less comfortable is the interaction between these static definitions of 'place' and the inherently dynamic innovation economies of the Fourth Industrial Revolution, and the 4.0 age.

This static understanding of place has, in turn, influenced the shape of a recent spate of 'place-based' policy approaches and has in some instances meant a retreat to an inward directionality, insularity and parochialism. Community Wealth Building (see Guinan et al. 2020), the latest 'place-based model to gain prominence, seeks to minimise wealth extraction from local economies and instead to generate local benefits through local procurement, re-investment in the local economy and community ownership models. While the approach has been successful in retaining spend in several adopting areas, the model can get stuck at the local procurement stage (arguably an easier policy to implement than the deeper move to community ownership) and, when it does, is one example of where a 'place-based' approach encourages an inward focus and flow.

'Place-based' approaches also tend to seek or prove 'embeddedness' in a place. Place-based innovation tends to focus on the acknowledged strengths of a place, which are often so called because they have a basis in a place's heritage. The deep and dynamic understanding of place employed in panonomics proposes that instead of evidencing a historical significance to a place, grounding, anchoring—and in many cases tethering—the place and its innovation capacity to the confines of its history, there is instead an opportunity to liberate and significantly enhance both place and innovation through the prioritisation of a distinctly cultural heritage, embracing the rich inter-complexities of a place's culture and its past, current and future dynamics.

Viewing the key concepts of 'place' and 'innovation' through a cultural heritage lens introduces the crucial and transformative factor of time. Time—the fourth dimension—is the key focal point and metric in the panonomic model. The COVID-19 pandemic has brutally distorted our understanding of time, of space and of how they interact. In the various lockdowns, time—our most precious commodity, the thing through which we express love and care, the thing which we are constantly trying to get more of and 'free up', and the thing which we buy and sell through our labour, has necessarily had to find a new meaning beyond its value in per-hour rates of labour. Notions of space too have been reconfigured with the advent of social distancing revealing the importance of personal and public space and creating new challenges for social interaction, connection and communication. Time has become a new narrative concept for space, with the advent of '15-minute cities', as proposed for Paris in Mayor Anne Hidalgo's 2020 re-election campaign, and a slightly more leisurely journey time as the basis for Scotland's '20-minute neighbourhoods' in its new national planning framework.

In essence, panonomics is a spatiotemporal model, but one which favours the concept of place over space (the difference between which is explored in further detail in Chapter 2), subverting the framing of the majority of spacetime models by giving time precedence over place in the spatiotemporal equation. Breaking out from the predominantly spatial narratives which dominated twentieth-century development, an approach which has continued over the first twenty years of the twenty-first century and which has brought with it hyper-development, agglomeration economies and, latterly the unstoppable rise (and adulteration) of 'place', panonomics proposes a new organisational model which prioritises and foregrounds time. Flipping the central premise of capital investment—the increase in value of a capital asset over time—on its head, the panonomic model recognises and prioritises the inherent value of time as our shared and most precious asset. Recognising space as a limited resource, panonomics proposes not that we 'Build Back Better' by eating further into available land mass, but that we direct progress onward and upward toward the infinite resource of time.

1.4 Innovating Toward a 'Future Now'

4.0 is an Innovation age, but our journey through it is stymied by a challenging paradox: Innovation has stopped innovating.

In his 2013 review of Europe's Smart Specialisation (S3) programme, a key tenet of the European Commission's strategic vision for an innovative Europe (and, since 2013, an ex-ante conditionality requirement for EU member states in receipt of funding), Christian Ketels laments a tendency for places to claim specialisms in 'bandwagon' sectors (EC 2013) such as biotechnology, digital and life sciences. In pursuing these limited specialisms, Ketels notes a reductionist, and as such flawed, application of S3 which in sharp contrast was initiated to support diversification by encouraging places to test out and explore their inherent innovation capacity and potential. Ketels' subsequent challenge for places to demonstrate 'an accent on fostering regional embeddedness' (Ketels 2013) remains as yet unmet and we continue to see the same 'bandwagon' sectors dominating innovation and specialism portfolios. A more recent critique of S3 includes commentary from Grillitsch (2016) who describes the process as having bee 'debased' by 'picking winners, rent-seeking behaviour, corruption and lock-ins' (Grillitsch 2016) and Hassink and Gong's assertion of 'delusion' in the selection of specialisms which they suggest are based on the demands of 'vested interest groups' (Hassink and Gong 2019).

The current status in innovation is further entrenched by the pressures of the free market economy and the elevation of competition over collaboration. Mimicking the fixed and bounded understandings of place, innovation has also become understood as a product, a noun, a thing, something which can be created and developed in laboratories on-site within fixed, bounded science parks and innovation districts and which is commercialised by universities in an (increasingly competitive) race to patent. This preoccupation with innovation as a product and ownership of patent severely restricts not only the exchange and interaction of ideas, an inherent factor in innovation as a dynamic process, but also the ability of innovation to meet our most pressing social challenges (as roundly demonstrated by the heavily commercialised, and as such limited, roll out of the COVID-19 vaccine).

In recognition of this innovation paradox, recent years have seen a marked rise in calls for more expansive approaches to innovation. Robert Madelin's 2016 paper for the European Commission on the future of innovation in Europe states explicitly that 'Innovation is more than science and technology. Social demand and needs-driven innovation matter more than ever'. (EC 2016). Schot and Steinmuller posit a new framing of transformative innovation policy in their 2018 paper for the UN, which they characterise as 'Innovation 3.0', oriented toward 'socio-technical system change' and attached to the UN's Sustainable Development Goals (Schot and Steinmuller 2018). Gabriel Rissola et al's 2017 report for the EC's Joint Research Centre advocates for dynamic, place-based innovation ecosystems and 'a quadruple helix paradigm (companies, research and innovation centres, the public administration and citizens) in the design and implementation of innovation strategies' (Rissola et al. 2017).

Rissola's report notes an assertion by Autio et al. (2014) that 'governments and national systems on innovation (NSA) have generally adopted policies and initiatives to stimulate innovation without paying sufficient attention to ***when*** and ***where*** entrepreneurs innovate' (Rissola et al. 2017). Dominique Foray, whose work has been seminal in the development of the Smart Specialisation concept in both theory and practice, reflects in a recent paper on the importance of the 'bottom-up component of the S3 approach' (Foray et al. 2020) and its centrality to the process of 'entrepreneurial discovery' (the act of finding a new product, purpose, resource or opportunity, as described in Kirzner 1997). This broad base understanding of innovation, both in terms of ***what*** innovation is and ***who*** has licence to innovate is explored in detail in a 2019 report, again led by Rissola, which asserts that the success of innovation ecosystems is dependent on the extent to which they are 'embedded in the social and spatial fine grain of places and encompass a diversity of actors' (Rissola et al. 2019).

This book includes further contextual exploration of questions around the when, where, who and what of 4.0 as an innovation economy, but contends that the critical questions in making further progress through 4.0 relate to the ***how*** and the ***why***. Panonomics presents a holistic and all-encompassing model which embraces a whole spectrum understanding of place and all of its facets, idiosyncrasies and complexities in answer to the question of how and asserts unreservedly the future survival of the human species and the planet through the collective accumulation of time as the why. Advocating for collective progress toward a shared mission, panonomics replaces the competition inherent in the free market economy with collectivism and collaboration which, combined with a deep and dynamic understanding of the concept of place, presents a framework in which innovation can once again be free to innovate. Applying a similarly deep and dynamic understanding to the concept of time, the panonomic model advocates for long-term thinking and embracing the notion of a 'Future Now', envisaging time as a series of successive futures (in which our present now is a past's future and in which each future is a future's now), and embracing the limitless potential of the infinite.

1.5 Summary: Presenting Panonomics

The COVID-19 pandemic has brutally distorted our relationship with both space and time, raising practical and existential questions about our contemporary way of life and the future of our species and the planet. Successive 'lockdowns' have seen the concept of time take on new meaning as 'time at the office' has become a thing of the past and time with our loved ones has become unavoidable for some and rarer and more precious for others. Notions of space too have been reconfigured with the advent of social distancing revealing the importance of personal and public space and creating new challenges for spatial planning and management.

The concept of 'place', which prior to the pandemic had already made a rapid ascension into policymaking in correlation with the devolution agenda and renewed calls for localism, has seen a recent re-emergence thanks in some part to the necessary lockdowns forcing an increased focus on immediate localities and consequently spurring a new wave of community-led initiatives and support for 'place-based' approaches.

Both the pandemic and the lockdowns have underscored the severe limitations of our current organisational model and in particular the systemic and structural inequalities inherent within the dominant western economic paradigm. Free market economics, based on a binary framework of supply and demand has failed to realise an adequate response to the pandemic and the universality of its challenges and needs.

This book presents panonomics as a new organisational paradigm. Reflecting its etymological root (from the Greek *pan* for 'all' and *nomos* for 'accounts'), the panonomic framework rejects the binaries, polarities and dichotomies of the dominant economic model and looks beyond the challenging compromises of the 'Third Way' middle-ground to instead propose a holistic and all-encompassing 'Fourth Way'. Presenting panonomics as a fit for purpose paradigm to support the re-innovation of innovation and our continued progress through 4.0 as an innovation age, the book explores key questions of the what, where, when, who and—crucially—the how and why of what this new systemic paradigm should look and feel like. Freeing the concepts of place and time from fixed and bounded understandings, panonomics presents the opportunity for innovation, liberation and our shared, collective and sustainable progress toward a 'Future Now'.

References

Autio, E, Kenney, M, Mustar, P, Siegel, D, & Wright, M (2014) Entrepreneurial innovation: The importance of context. *Research Policy*, *43*(7), 1097–1108. https://doi.org/10.1016/j.respol.2014.01.015.

Blakely, G (2019) Stolen: How to Save the World from Financialisation. London: Verso.

EC (2013) 'The Role of Clusters in Smart Specialisation Strategies'. DG Research & Innovation. Luxembourg: Publications Office of the European Union.

EC (2016) 'Opportunity Now: Europe's Mission to Innovate', ESRC Strategic Notes prepared by Madelin. R, 5th July. Luxembourg: Publications Office of the European Union.

Foray, D, Eichler, M, and Keller, M (2020). Smart Specialization Strategies—Insights Gained From a Unique European Policy Experiment on Innovation and Industrial Policy Design. Review of Evolutionary Political Economy. London: Springer.

Giddens, A (1991) The Third Way: The Renewal of Social Democracy. London: Wiley.

Grillitsch, M (2016). 'Institutions, Smart Specialisation Dynamics and Policy', Environment and Planning C: Government and Policy Volume 34, 22–37.

Guinan, J, Mcinroy, N, Liebowitz, J, and McklInley, S (2020) Owning the Future: After Covid-19, A New Era of Community Wealth Building. Manchester: CLES.

Hassink, R, and Gong, H (2019) Six Critical Questions About Smart Specialization. Taylor & Francis.

Harvey, D (2001) Spaces of Capital: Towards a Critical Geography. London: Routledge.

Hickel, J (2020) Less is More. London: Penguin Random House.

Hoekstra, R et al. (2020) Measuring the Wellbeing Economy: How to Go Beyond-GDP, Wellbeing Economy Alliance.

Jackson, T (2009) Prosperity Without Growth. London: Routledge.

Kallis, G, Paulson, S, D'alisa, G, and Demaria, F (2020) The Case for Degrowth. Cambridge: Polity.

Kelly, M (2013) Toward a Generative Economy. Open Democracy. Accessed 4 July 2021.

Ketels, C (2013) The Role of Clusters in Smart Specialisation Strategies. DG Research & Innovation. Luxembourg: Publications Office of the European Union.

Kleibrink A, Gianelle C, and Doussineau M (2016) 'Monitoring Innovation and Territorial Development in Europe: Emergent Strategic Management', European Planning Studies. https://doi.org/10.1080/09654313.2016.1181717.

Mazzucato, M (2017) The Entrepreneurial State. London: Penguin.
Mazzucato, M (2021) Mission Economy. London: Penguin.
OECD (2011) Towards Green Growth in Emerging Market Economies. https://www.oecd-ilibrary.org/environment/towards-green-growth-in-emerging-market-economies_d5e5b5d7-en. Accessed 4 July 2021.
Perez, C (2016) Capitalism, Technology and a Green Global Golden Age. London: IIPP.
Raworth, K (2017) Doughnut Economics London: Random House.
Rissola, G, Hervás, F, Slavcheva, M, and Jonkers, K (2017) Place-Based Innovation Ecosystems: Espoo Innovation Garden and Aalto University (Finland). Luxembourg: Publications Office of the European Union.
Rissola, G, (editor), Bevilacqua, C, Monardo, B, and Trillo, C. (2019) Place-Based Innovation Ecosystems: Boston-Cambridge Innovation Districts (USA). Luxembourg: Publications Office of the European Union.
RSA (2017) Inclusive Growth Commission. https://www.thersa.org/projects/archive/public-services-communities/inclusive-growth-commission. Accessed 4 July 2021.
Scharmer, C.O (2016) Theory U: Leading from the Future as it Emerges. Oakland: Berrett-Koehler Publishers.
Schot, J, and Steinmueller, W.E (2018) Three Frames for Innovation Policy: R&D, Systems of Innovation and Transformative Change. Elsevier
Schwab, K (2016) The Fourth Industrial Revolution. London: Penguin.
Soja, E (1996) Thirdspace: Journeys to Los Angeles and Other Real-and-Imagined Places. Oxford: Blackwell.
Trebeck, K, and Williams, J (2019) The Economics of Arrival: Ideas for A Grown-Up Economy. Bristol: Bristol University Press.
World Bank (2020) Global Economic Prospects, June 2020. Washington, DC: World Bank. https://doi.org/10.1596/978-1-4648-1553-9. License: Creative Commons Attribution CC BY 3.0 IGO.
World Economic Forum (2016) The 10 skills you need to thrive in the Fourth Industrial Revolution. Accessed 4 July 2021.
World Economic Forum (2017) Advancing Human-Centred Economic Progress.

CHAPTER 2

Foundation in Place: 'The Where'

Abstract The panonomic model is founded on a deep and comprehensive understanding of the concept of place, which is plotted as the horizontal axis of its core framework. Building on the well-established scientific and mathematical concept of 'spacetime', panonomics is conceived in essence as a 'placetime' model, in which place is presented as distinct to the concept of space and in which the distinctive characteristics of place are emphasised. While traditional innovation strategies have tended to adopt place-blind, place-based or—at best—place-grounded approaches, this chapter charts the interrelated development of the concept of 'Smart Specialisation' in innovation policy and the emerging practice of placemaking. Panonomics is presented as a place-driven model which further advances on these approaches by fully embracing a whole-spectrum understanding of place, which is deeply embedded in the cultural heritage and distinct characteristics of a particular place. Proposing a directionality of moving upward and outward from the place, rather than restricted to a place, the model can be applied at any scale and as such offers place as both a connective tissue and dynamic foundation for collective advancement toward local, regional, national and global goals.

Keywords Place · Space · Placemaking · Innovation · Cultural Heritage · Embeddedness

C. Devaney, *Panonomics*,
https://doi.org/10.1007/978-3-030-87509-1_2

2.1 Introduction: Place, Placemaking and Panonomics

In the UK, the concept of place started to gain notable traction as a policy driver in the late 2000s, bolstered by an embryonic devolution agenda and the introduction of regional development agencies, alongside a post-2008 backlash against globalism, rising calls for localism and stronger powers and budgetary control for local authorities. Those calls have only grown stronger during the successive years of austerity that have followed (not just in the UK, but in the US and several countries across Europe) with ever-increasing competition for ever-more limited funding. Around 2014, as opportunities around UK devolution, and in particular the chance for regional governance under 'Metro Mayors' began to emerge (linked to the work of the RSA's 2013 City Growth Commission), there was a huge push for city-regions to assert themselves as being deemed capable of self-governance, bringing about a whole new layer of 'place' narratives as those city-regions set out their stall.

The distinct, but related, practice of 'placemaking' has its roots in the seminal work of Jane Jacobs in the 1960s onward in which she focussed on urban design and the urgent need to respect and retain the character of places in what she saw as a relentless pursuit of a heavily sanitised and prescriptive 'urban order', and in the work of Jan Gehl from the 1970s onward, a leading advocate for 'in between spaces' and of the primacy of people and pedestrians in urban spatial planning.

Placemaking has gained significant following and traction in recent years and is now a global—and commercially active movement. Like heritage, which so often finds itself subsumed into a tourism agenda, contemporary iterations of place and the practice of 'placemaking' have arguably been rolled into an outward-facing 'place marketing'. In both cases, the result can feel like something which is focussed primarily on people who are *not* from the place in question, rather than those who are. The RSA's programme of work around 'Heritage, Identity and Place', delivered in partnership with the National Heritage Lottery Fund, has contributed to a developing richness in the place narrative, and particularly (as the title of its programme suggests), in exploring the deep connections between people's sense of place and their personal and collective heritage and identity. In its 2014 provocation for the research programme, the RSA posits that the agent is unclear in the concept of placemaking, and that it is 'unclear who or what is doing the making, or who should be' (RSA 2014). While it may have become clearer in recent years who is doing the making, the jury is still out on who should be, with various players and actors exerting various levels of influence on the spatial, commercial and cultural aspects of place. Is there a place in placemaking for everyone?

The panonomic model responds in the affirmative. Where previous approaches to placemaking have in many cases been ignorant to the indigenous people and communities of places, resulting in marginalisation and displacement, and in many cases too have attempted to recreate or orchestrate a new cultural expression for the place in the guise of regeneration, panonomics is founded on a whole spectrum understanding of place which embraces all characteristics of that place within its scope. This understanding of place is one which is embedded in the cultural heritage of that place and its people. Panonomics proposes that each place brings a unique contribution toward the shared mission and envisages a 'place-driven' organisational model, which encompasses and draws on the whole human creativity, knowledge, skills and life experience of that place.

Panonomics is a model for an innovation economy, designed to meet the needs of The Fourth Industrial Revolution and the 4.0 age. Just as placemaking is vulnerable to the mores of the market in realising the vision of property developers, resulting in many cases in bland and ill-fitting development with little resonance with the cultural heritage of the place, so innovation has been stymied by a competitive and market-driven paradigm. Prioritising competition over collaboration, profit over progress, and blinded further by the dogged pursuit of 'bandwagon' (Ketels 2013) sectors such as digital and biotechnology and the creation of facsimile innovation hubs and districts; innovation has stopped innovating. By creating a space in which a full spectrum of place-driven creativity, knowledge and life experience can be brought together in collaboration toward a collective and progressive mission, panonomics offers a systemic model in which innovation can be re-innovated.

2.2 Space and Place: What's the Difference?

Panonomics is founded on the concept of place, as distinct to space. It employs a similar structure to the well-established concept of spacetime which, in physics and mathematics, describes any model which incorporates the three physical dimensions of space (height, breadth and depth) with the fourth dimension of time. These dimensions and their effects on perception and experience are fundamental to human perceptions and experiences of life. As a result, many of our organisational models and frameworks plot space and time as key axes. The organisation of capital economies measures, for example, the performance of space as a capital asset (primarily in the form of land) in terms of its monetary value over time. David Harvey describes the related capitalist economic phenomenon of globalisation as 'the annihilation of space over time' (Harvey 2017).

In *Space and Place* (1977), the celebrated human geographer Yi Fu Tuan asserts that the concepts of 'space' and 'place' require each other for definition. 'From the security and stability of place', Tuan writes, 'we are aware of the openness, freedom, and threat of space, and vice versa'. (Tuan 1977).

The notion of 'space' and its definition, concept, structure, physical manifest, material forms, relational properties and existential meanings have a philosophical provenance stretching back to Ancient Greece, to Socrates, Plato's *Timaeus* and Aristotle's *Physics*. Fundamental to the physical universe, space features prominently in the works of Da Vinci, the discourse of the Renaissance and in the major works of physicists and mathematicians, including Newton and Einstein. Space is integral to a number of philosophical schools, featuring for example in the work of early twentieth-century structuralists such as Bertrand Russell, and later in Barthes, Derrida, Foucault, Baudrillard and the post-structuralists. Its literary provenance can be seen in the late sixteenth and early seventeenth-century works of John Donne and the metaphysical poets, and in the prominent spatial contexts of the nineteenth-century Lake Poets (Wordsworth, Taylor-Coleridge) and the First World War poets (Owen, Sassoon, Brooke). It is a notion of significant and particular influence in nineteenth and early twentieth-century American literature, as reflected throughout the modern American literary canon, from Melville's cartography of the Pacific coast and its ocean 'spaces that before were blank' in *Moby Dick* (Melville 1851/2012) to the evocative landscapes of T.S. Eliot's *The Waste Land* (1922), F. Scott Fitzgerald's *The Great Gatsby* (1925), and Kerouac's *On the Road* in which 'all that raw land rolls in one unbelievable huge bulge over to the West Coast' (Kerouac 1957/1991).

As might be expected, both space and place are key tenets in geography, which has its roots as an academic discipline in the idiographic study of countries and continents and a typological, descriptive study of their landscapes. Like many of its artistic and literary counterparts, the scientific and academic merit of geography, and particularly the development of 'human geography' as a distinctly more qualitative branch of study, was called into question in the late 1940s to mid-1950s America and (along with Kerouac and the other Beat Generation poets and writers) was subject to the scrutiny and censorship of McCarthyism (aligned with Cold War anti-communism and so-called 'Red Scare'). This censure resulted in the cancellation of geography as a subject of study at Harvard, in 1948, and contributed to the 'Quantitative Revolution' (Adams 2013) of the 1960s. The Quantitative Revolution marked a paradigm shift in academic discipline of geography, which saw the construct and adoption of laws, theories mathematical techniques and statistical modelling methods, recasting geography as a nomothetic 'spatial science'. Emphasising in particular the concepts of distance, direction and connection, this scientific approach conceptualised the idea of 'absolute space' (Massey 1996) and of space as 'objective, empirical and mappable' (Hubbard et al. 2004).

A counter-revolution in the late 1970s, aligned with a rise in political activism and the emergence of the anti-war, environmental and human rights movements, foregrounded 'radical geography' as a prominent subfield, which in turn gave rise to 'critical geography', a branch connected to Marxist, feminist, postmodern, post-structural, queer and left-wing ideologies. Critical geography is characterised by the rejection of empiricism and positivism, and an acknowledgement of, and focus on, the spatial dynamics of power and oppression (Kitchin and Hubbard 1999). The work of Yi Fu Tuan has been pivotal in foregrounding human (and humanistic) geography as a key branch of critical geography and Tuan was among the pioneers, alongside Relph (*Place and Placenessness*, 1976), Buttimer (*The Human Experience of Space and Place*, 1976) and others, of elevating the concept of 'place' within spatial discourse. The 'spatial turn' in the decade which followed, a term denoting a perceptible shift in the arts, literary studies and the social sciences toward spatial analysis during the 1980s (Guldi 2011), is observable in the work of Foucault, Lefebvre and Soja, a phenomenon which has since been further consolidated by the advent of digital mapping tools since the mid-1990s, notably GIS (Geographic Information System mapping), leading Crang and Thrift to observe that 'space is the everywhere of modern thought' (Crang and Thrift 2000).

Focussing on human experience of and human relationships to, with and within place and space, Tuan's extensive body of work explores humanistic approaches through a series of dialectics which include *Continuity and Discontinuity* (1984), *Morality and Imagination* (1989) and, notably *Space and Place* (1977). In *Space and Place*, Tuan explores what he describes as the 'opposing pulls' between space and place, and a related opposition between 'intimacy and distance' (Tuan 1977). He describes a deeply subjective, sensory experience of space, positing that: 'Human beings not only discern geometric patterns in nature and create abstract spaces in the mind, but they also try to embody their feelings, images, and thoughts in tangible material. The result is sculptural and architectural space, and on a large scale, the planned city'. Place, he says, is 'a type of object. Places and objects define space, giving it a geometric personality', adding a temporal consideration to the distinct between space and place by posting that 'if we think of space as that which allows movement, then place is pause; each pause in movement makes it possible for location to be transformed into place' (Tuan 1977).

At its simplest, Tuan says, place can be expressed as 'location plus meaning' (Tuan 1977). As we look toward emergence from the pandemic and its lockdowns, a period which has been referred to as 'The Great Pause' (see Janoo and Bone-Dodds 2020), there is a point-in-time opportunity to reflect on a collective location and meaning, and to transform the conceptual and space that we share into a shared place.

2.3 Place and Placemaking

The process of placemaking also draws on the work of Tuan, with a literal application of his assertion that 'Places and objects define space' (Tuan 1977). Placemaking is described by one of its chief proponents, the Project for Public Spaces (PPS) as 'a collaborative process by which we can shape our public realm in order to maximize shared value' (PPS 2007). PPS, who adopted 'placemaking' as an overarching term for its practice in 1991, advocates for 'Lighter, Quicker, Cheaper' intervention, which 'views a place in its entirety' and which champions 'function over form' (PPS 2007). Like its root of 'place', the notion of placemaking has been rapidly integrated into policy and practice, with a particular ascendance in the years post-2008. Placemaking has been described as having a 'mirage'-like quality, which 'is why it is so attractive to so many' (Legge 2015). It is this incompleteness that compelled The Royal Society of Arts (RSA) to posit a critical question about the practice: 'In the act of placemaking, who or what is doing the making? Who should be?' (RSA 2014).

Describing placemaking as 'the shared reclamation of space', Wouter Jan Verheul (2017) gives his answer to the RSA's question when he describes how placemaking is supported by a 'triangular relationship between governments, the business community and civil society'. As what he calls the 'shared reclamation of space', Verheul asserts placemaking as the antidote to Zukin's theory of 'McDonaldsization', in which Zukin observes that 'places are turning into everywhere else' (Zukin 2010). Verheul puts forward four forms of placemaking: ***social*** placemaking, focussed on social tasks and community building (through, for example, communal baking and eating), ***cultural*** placemaking, 'in which a place is given new identity', ***economic*** placemaking, focussed on 'increasing the value of a place and its surroundings', and ***innovative*** placemaking, a sub-set of economic placemaking, focussed on 'the idea that a diversity of people with their own knowledge and competences will lead to new innovations and that public space will play a major role' (Verheul 2017).

2.4 Place and Innovation

Innovation, defined in the Organization for Economic Cooperation and Development (OECD) as 'the implementation of a new or significantly improved product (good or service), or process, a new marketing method, or a new organizational method in business practices, workplace organization or external relations' (OECD 2005) has, as noted in Kotsemir et al. (2013), 'evolved as the synonym for the development of nations, technological progress and driver of business success. Innovation nowadays is not simply the "creation of something new" but also a panacea for the solution of board range of problems'. (Kotsemir et al. 2013).

A portfolio of work from The Brookings Institute's Bass Initiative has been pivotal in framing emerging thinking around the interconnectivity between innovation and placemaking. Katz and Wagner (2014) assert a typology based around three models of 'innovation districts' in cities: the 'anchor plus' model, in which a clustering of assets and infrastructure occurs around the presence of an anchor institution, such as a university; the 're-imagined urban areas model', in which former industrial or warehousing sites undergo large-scale regeneration (often, Katz and Wagner observe, to be found in historic waterfront districts); and the 'urbanized science park' model, which sees new industry and commercial activity in suburban or ex-urban areas growing around clustered scientific activity.

In a later review of this predominantly spatial analysis of innovation strategy, Katz et al. (2015) introduce 'the imperative to combine and activate physical assets in ways that create vibrant "places"', quoting Ethan Kent, Chief Executive of the Project for Public Spaces (PPS)' description of place as 'environments in which people have invested meaning over time. A place has its own history—a unique cultural and social identity that is defined by the way it is used and the people who use it'. (Katz et al. 2015).

Place has been a key tenet in European innovation policy since the work of the European Commission's 2009 Knowledge for Growth Expert Group and its recommendation which led to the development and introduction of Smart Specialisation, a policy framework designed to enhance the innovation capacity of a nominated place by 'entrepreneurial discovery' of new specialisms, opportunities and competencies (Foray 2015). Since 2013, it has been a compulsory ex-ante conditionality requirement for EU member states and regions accessing EU funds to have a Smart Specialisation Strategy (S3) (EC 2013).

2.5 Place and Smart Specialisation

Place is implicit in the level of granularity required by Smart Specialisation. While there is clear ideological synergy between the regional focus of S3 and the place-based approach, 'Smart Specialisation Strategies…were initially developed from an a-spatial concept (and) have needed to be reworked and redefined in the context of regional analysis' (Ketels 2013). Ketels' influential 2013 report for the European Commission advocates for regionally distinct, place-based approaches to S3, as opposed to 'place-blind interventions', setting out the desired logic for S3 delivery which prioritises regional context, participation and ownership and place-specific future visioning. The report identifies a lack of stakeholder engagement, insufficient analysis of regional assets and a 'Tendency for regional strategies to chase the same "bandwagon" sectors' (Ketels 2013) as key S3 policy flaws.

The co-relation between place and S3 is made explicit by the 2009 Barca report (and restated by McCann 2015). The Barca report defines a place-based approach as 'a long-term strategy aimed at tackling persistent underutilization of potential and reducing persistent social exclusion in specific places through external interventions and multi-level governance' (Barca 2009). While this is a useful definition, and of its time, both

S3 and place-based concepts have since continued to evolve, and whilst the concept of 'place' remains 'incompletely developed' (RSA 2014), in emerging just ahead of the place-based paradigm, S3 has been able to respond to and absorb a deepening understanding of what 'place' means.

2.6 Place, Innovation and Cultural Heritage

Place-based innovation, including S3, tends to focus on the acknowledged strengths of a place. Often, these strengths are so acknowledged because they have a basis in a place's industrial or cultural heritage (as noted in Rissola et al. 2017). The city-region of Greater Manchester in the UK, for example, focussed its 2013–20 Smart Specialisation strategy on its innovation capacity in advanced manufacture, and in particular its pioneering work in the development of Graphene, building on its recognised heritage as an industrial centre for manufacturing (GMCA 2013).

Mirroring fixed and static understandings of place, the concept of a place's heritage tends to be attached to its built heritage, a response both demonstrated and influenced by the 1972 UNESCO World Heritage Convention definition of 'cultural heritage' as monuments, groups of buildings and sites (UNESCO 1972). In 1994, the ICOMOS Nara Document called for cultural context in regard to permanence, recognising, for example, the cultural heritage value—but impermanence—of ritually rebuilt wooden temples and mud huts (and, for an instance of significant scale, the temporary cities built as part of the Hindu Kumbh Mela festival celebrations), pioneering a school of thought which has since introduced a more fluid understanding of heritage, particularly in regard to cultural heritage, underscored by the formal recognition of 'intangible cultural heritage' by UNESCO in 2003. UNESCO defines intangible cultural heritage as 'traditions or living expressions inherited from our ancestors and passed on to our descendants, such as oral traditions, performing arts, social practices, rituals, festive events, knowledge and practices concerning nature and the universe or the knowledge and skills to produce traditional crafts', and asserts that its protection is integral to maintaining cultural diversity and supporting cultural dialogue. UNESCO highlights that intangible cultural heritage can be past or contemporary, is inclusive and representative and community based. It 'can only be heritage when it is recognized as such by the communities, groups or individuals that create, maintain and transmit it—without their recognition, nobody else can decide for them that a given expression or practice is their heritage' (UNESCO 2003) This thinking continues to influence contemporary cultural heritage research, such as the Royal Society of Arts' advocacy for community-based 'Networked Heritage' and 'Heritage Citizens' in its portfolio of work around 'Heritage, Identity and Place' (RSA 2017a).

The relationship between cultural heritage and innovation is a relatively fresh research domain. From a policy perspective, where a relationship is noted, the focus tends to be on the economic value of cultural heritage, principally through tourism. The report of the EC Horizon 2020 expert group on cultural heritage (EC 2015) sets out a framework for cultural heritage in Europe. The report asserts that 'modest investment in cultural heritage can pay substantial dividends… economically but also in terms of improving environmental sustainability and social cohesion'. (EC 2015) and argues that 'the European Union should vigorously promote the innovative use of cultural heritage for economic growth and jobs, social cohesion and environmental sustainability'. (EC 2015). Notably, the focus here is on 'innovative use' of culture to generate value, rather than the inherent value of culture, or cultural value as a driver of place and innovation.

2.7 Embeddedness and Dynamism

A common denominator between place, innovation and cultural heritage can be found in the concept of 'embeddedness'. Ketels, as previously noted, calls for 'an accent on fostering regional embeddedness' (Ketels 2013) in his 2013 review of European S3 and cluster policy. The call is made in mitigation of a number of noted policy flaws, principally the tendency for regions to choose 'bandwagon' sectors, such as digital and bioscience, as S3 specialisms. The Ketels report marks a pivotal point in the development of Smart Specialisation, and in the developing place paradigm, as both move from superficially place-based strategies to strategies embedded and demonstrably grounded in place. The emergence of these place-grounded approaches has been marked in recent years by a notable rise in the number and prominence of social enterprises and in voluntary and 'third sector' activity.

The concept of embeddedness is widely attributed to the work of Karl Polanyi, principally *The Great Transformation* (1944/1991), although a number of commentator's also point to its occurrence too in the earlier work of Polanyi's contemporary, Richard Thurnwald (see Beckert 2007).

Polanyi's substantivist model of embeddedness asserts that rather than being manifest as a separate and distinct sphere, the economy is embedded not just in economic institutions, but in all manner of social and cultural norms, moral concerns, politics and religion. Polanyi's model is based on non-capitalist, pre-industrial economies which, he says, are based not only on market forces but also on redistribution and reciprocity. In one of only two occasions which Polanyi explicitly mentions the term, he describes the importance and nature of 'bartering' and long-term relationships in embedded exchange systems, observing that: 'In the vast ancient systems of redistribution, acts of barter as well as local markets were a usual but not more than a subordinate trait. The same is true where reciprocity rules: Acts of barter are here usually embedded in long-range relations implying trust and confidence, a situation which tends to obliterate the bilateral character of the transaction' (Polanyi 1944/1991).

Returning to Ketel's call for embeddedness in S3 (Ketels 2013), there is some tension between fixed (spatial and socio-economic) definitions of place and the historical anchoring and institutional (church, state) dominance present in the substantivist paradigm of embeddedness on the one hand, and the 'dynamic processes' of innovation ecosystems (Rissola et al. 2017), short-term risk-taking, learning, regenerative shedding and redefinition of priorities that is actively encouraged in the process of Smart Specialisation (Foray 2015) on the other. This regenerative process in support of economic systems has a long and rich provenance, dating from Schumpeter's 'gale of creative destruction', the 'process of industrial mutation that incessantly revolutionizes the economic structure from within' (Schumpeter 1942) and its rise to policy prominence in the 1950s. More recently, Schumpeter's influence can be seen in Harvey's 'spatial fix' (2001), Castells' 'space of flows' (2010), and in the explicit incorporation of 'creative destruction' as a key driver in Smart Specialisation itself (Foray 2015). The tension arises when these spatial dynamics are considered alongside the deep and immovable social. historical and moral structures asserted as foundations of embeddedness, as present in the substantivist model.

A better fit can arguably be found in the sociological, neo-substantivist paradigm around embeddedness brought forward by Granovetter (1985), the central tenet of which is based on the theory of individual economic agency being 'embedded in concrete, ongoing systems of social relations' (Granovetter 1985). Granovetter introduced this understanding in direct reference to an ongoing debate between substantivists and formalists in economic anthropology and two competing concepts of action in sociology, in which actors where either ‘undersocialized’, isolated economic units or ‘oversocialized’, entirely controlled by social norms. Granovetter’s definition, put forward as a third alternative, promotes a structuralist economic sociology in which economic outcomes are explained by the structural (‘concrete’) properties of social networks (Beckert 2007).

Beckert 2007 observes that Granovetter’s central idea of ‘the network’ ‘has become the most influential advance within the new economic sociology’ but argues that this understanding of embeddedness is far removed from the original meaning of the term put forward by Polanyi. Polanyi’s work, Beckert says, is ‘rooted in institutional analysis’ (Beckert 2007). In short, Polanyi’s work explores networked relations between institutions, while Granovetter’s definition focuses on the network itself. The delicate balance present in Granovetter’s definition, in which networks of social relations are at once concrete and dynamic, resonates well with the required—and in some cases, evident—relationship between place and innovation. Application of this more fluid and arguably culturally aware definition of embeddedness has implications for the understanding of both place and innovation, and challenges activity emerging within the place/innovation nexus to respond.

2.8 Summary: Panonomics: A Place-Driven Model

There is a clear tension between the fixed, static and bounded (primarily spatial and socio-economic) definitions which are widely applied to ‘place’ and the inherent fluidity and dynamism of the innovation process. Historically, this tension has been alleviated—and arguably avoided—by employing only a very superficial understanding and expression of place in the development of innovation spaces. ‘Urbanized science parks’, the first typology of innovation district identified by Katz and Wagner (2014) and still the stereotypical ‘go to’ for places in terms of spatial planning for innovation, have traditionally shown little resonance with place and often maintain both a cultural isolation and geographical distance from their respective urban cores.

Rather than attaching the confines of place to innovation, panonomics proposes that a better approach to alleviating the tension between the fixed parameters of place and the dynamics of innovation is to instead pursue a more dynamic, deeper and culturally aware understanding and practice of place. This deep expression of place is presented as the foundation of panonomics as a place-driven organisational model. Adopting an upward and outward directionality, that is, emerging from the place, the place-driven principle can be applied at any scale and as such can operate as the foundation for progress toward local, regional, national and global goals. Where previously, innovation and economic development strategies have tended to focus only on those aspects of place identified as key assets or strengths, panonomics proposes a holistic and comprehensive understanding of place which encompasses and draws on the whole human creativity, knowledge, skills and life experience of that place. In doing so, panonomics creates a space for new relationships, collaboration and knowledge exchange, enabling application of place-driven innovation capacity to social challenges and resulting in the re-innovation of innovation.

References

Adams, JS (2013) The Quantitative Revolution in Urban Geography. Taylor and Francis.

Beckert, J (2007) The Great Transformation of Embeddedness Karl Polanyi and the New Economic Sociology. Cologne: Max Planck Institute for the Study of Societies Cologne.

Castells, M (2010) The Rise of the Network Society. London: Wiley & Blackwell.

Crang, M, and Thrift, N (2000) Thinking Space. London: Routledge.

GMCA (2013) Greater Manchester, Towards A RIS3 Strategy. Accessed 4 July 2021.

Granovetter, M (1985) 'Economic Action and Social Structure, the Problem of Embeddedness', American Journal of Sociology Volume 91, Issue 3. Chicago. University of Chicago Press.

Foray, D (2015) Smart Specialisation: Opportunities and Challenges for Regional Innovation Policy. London: Routledge.

Guldi, J (2011) What is the Spatial Turn? Scholars Lab—University of Virginia.

Harvey, D (2001) Spaces of Capital: Towards a Critical Geography. London: Routledge.

Harvey, D (2017) Marx, Capital and the Madness of Economic Reason. London: Profile.

Hubbard, P, Kitchin, R, and Valentine, G (2004) Key Thinkers on Space and Place. London: Sage.

Janoo, A, and Bone-Dodds, G (2020) The Great Pause. Open Democracy: The Great Pause | openDemocracy

Katz, B, and Wagner, J (2014) The Rise of Innovation Districts: A New Geography of Innovation in America. Washington: Brookings.
Katz, B, Vey JS, and Wagner, J (2015) One Year After: Observations on the Rise of Innovation Districts. Washington: Brookings.
Kerouac, J (1957/1991) On the Road. London: Penguin.
Ketels, C (2013) The Role of Clusters in Smart Specialisation Strategies. DG Research & Innovation, Luxembourg: Publications Office of the European Union.
Kitchin, R, and Hubbard, P (1999) Research, Action and Critical Geographies. London: Royal Geographical Society.
Kotsemir, M, Abroskin, A, and Dirk, M (2013) Innovation Concepts and Typology—An Evolutionary Discussion. Moscow: National Research University Higher School of Economics.
Legge, K (2015) The Evolution of Placemaking, in EDGE Condition, Vol.5. https://issuu.com/edgecondition/docs/edgecondition_vol5_placemaking_jan1.
Massey, D (1996) Politicising Space and Place. Taylor and Francis.
McCann, P (2015) The Regional and Urban Policy of the European Union: Cohesion, Results-Orientation and Smart Specialisation. Cheltenham: Edward Elgar.
Melville, H (1851/2012) Moby Dick. London: Penguin.
Polanyi, K (1944/1991) The Great Transformation. Boston: Beacon Press.
Rissola, G, Hervás, F, Slavcheva, M, and Jonkers, K (2017) Place-Based Innovation Ecosystems: Espoo Innovation Garden and Aalto University (Finland), Luxembourg: Publications Office of the European Union.
RSA (2014) A Place for Heritage. London: The Royal Society of Arts and the Heritage Lottery Fund.
Schumpeter, J (1942) Capitalism, Socialism and Democracy. New York: Harper & Brothers.
Tuan, YF (1977) Space and Place: The Perspective of Experience. Minneapolis: University of Minnesota Press.
UNESCO (1972) Convention Concerning the Protection of the World Cultural and Natural Heritage. https://whc.unesco.org/en/conventiontext/. Accessed 4 July 2021.
UNESCO (2003) What is Cultural Heritage? Accessed 4 July 2021.
Verheul, WJ (2017) Placemaking and the Discourse of the Public Place. Accessed 4 July 2021.
Zukin, S (2010) The Cultures of Cities. London: Wiley-Blackwell.

CHAPTER 3

A Fourth Way: 'The How'

Abstract Introducing 'A Fourth Way' as a conceptual framework for the new panonomic paradigm. 'A Fourth Way' is based on the theoretical concept of a fourth space, which is presented as a successor to the established and primarily post-structuralist theoretical concept of third space. The concept of a fourth space proposes that we look beyond the binaries and polarities which dominate our current organisational systems, and that we also reject the false consensus of the middle ground, to instead pursue and embrace an all-encompassing and holistic approach. 'A Fourth Way' applies these principles to policymaking and is presented as a successor to the favoured neoliberal ideology characterised as 'The Third Way'. This chapter sets out the literary provenance of third space theory, and the social and policy history of 'The Third Way' as contextual background, proposing that expansion beyond the constrictions of binary and tripartite approaches and adoption instead of 'A Fourth Way' and its holistic principles holds the key to sustainable progress and continued advancement through the 4.0 age.

Keywords A Fourth way · Fourth space · Third space · Third way · Sustainability · 4.0

C. Devaney, *Panonomics*,
https://doi.org/10.1007/978-3-030-87509-1_3

3.1 Introduction—A Fourth Way

The human experience is shaped by a deep historical, social, cultural, theoretical and literary tradition of tripartite structures, social and cultural reference points, systems and models, incorporating everything from three spatial dimensions (height, breadth and depth), Lefebvre's '*rhythmanalysis*' of 'space-time-energy' (Lefebvre 1992), Heidegger's three *ecstaces* of time (Heidegger 1927/2019), Foucault's *heterotopias* (a 'third space' between real and imagined') (Foucault 1986), Soja's trialectics of 'Third Space' (Soja 1996) to, more prosaically, 'A,B,C', 'top, middle and bottom', 'left, right and centre', *The Three Little Pigs* (Halliwell-Phillips 1842), Dumas' *Three Musketeers* (1844), the Holy Trinity, a footballing 'hat-trick' and Anthony Gidden's *The Third Way* (1991).

'A Fourth Way' asserts a next, and fourth, level of thinking, practice and human experience. It is based on a new theory of a fourth space, presented as a successor to the well-established, and primarily post-structural, theoretical concept of third space. Post-structuralist theory asserts that all binaries are based on hypothetical constructs and complex power dynamics which in delineating two points as opposite not only results in 'othering' (Lacan 1955), but also produces boundaries, peripheries, margins and a centre ground (Derrida 1972). This centre is opened up and explored as an intersecting 'third space' in the work of Bhabha (1994), Soja (1996), Foucault (1986) and a number of post-structuralist thinkers.

The concept of a fourth space extends this action further to propose an all-encompassing and holistic—as opposed to intersecting—space in which previously polarised concepts can be brought together in a meta-layered space. Fourth space transcends the delineated boundaries of separation identified by Derrida (1972)—and, with it, the centre, peripheries and margins—and as such can accommodate conceptually 'opposed' characteristics, as observed, for example, in Granovetter's understanding of 'embeddedness' as 'concrete, ongoing systems of social relations' (Granovetter 1985).

Encompassing and embodying this notion of a dynamic embeddedness, 'A Fourth Way' applies the holistic principles of this fourth space theory to policymaking and practice. As a policymaking tool, it is presented as a successor to the favoured neoliberal paradigm of 'The Third Way' (Giddens 1991). 'A Fourth Way' rejects both established binaries and polarities and the unstable consensus of the middle ground to instead embrace a holistic approach. 'A Fourth Way' is an expansive and progressive conceptual framework, which underpins the panonomic model by revealing and articulating a deep and comprehensive understanding of the key panonomic concepts of place and time. In bringing forward this holistic, fourth space, it also presents a new paradigm through which a whole range of established tripartite structures can be elevated.

Liberating fixed and, in some cases, paradoxical spatial and temporal dynamics beyond delineated polarities, boundaries and the centre ground, 'A Fourth Way' presents the challenge of '4' to the established 1,2,3 and a 'D' to the A,B,C. It is a D'Artagnan to *The Three Musketeers* and 'The Big, Bad Wolf' to *The Three Little Pigs.*

Without those catalytic fourth characters as antagonists, would those classic stories even exist?

3.2 Third Space

The concept of a third space has its roots in post-structuralism. The post-structuralist school critiques the structural semiotics of 'signs and signifiers' (Saussure 1916/1983), maintaining that all binary systems (truth/fiction, subject/object, real/unreal, God/man) are based on hypothetical constructs determined by power dynamics which, in producing recognised 'centres' also create boundaries and margins. Key post-structural thinkers whose vast bodies of work reference 'the other' and the process of othering include Derrida, Hegel, Freud, Sartre and—notably—Lacan.

Michel Foucault's analysis of established binary constructs goes a step further to not only observe 'the other', but to propose that these binaries are paradoxical. In '*The Order of Things*' (Foucault 1973), Foucault notes the dominance of 'Western' scientific ideas and practices since the eighteenth century and their resultant othering of 'non-normal' people who are deemed in those terms to be insane or perverted. Foucault's analysis of *heterotopias* (Foucault 1986), 'other places' such as prisons, brothels, ships, cemeteries and bars, is aligned to the concept of utopias and dystopias in which a third space is presented as an approximation or 'mirror' of a utopia, in order to allow the utopia to exist. Through using the concept of the mirror as a metaphor, Foucault creates a space that is at once real and imaginary (a reflection of a utopia, 'a placeless place'), articulating several types of heterotopias which exhibit this inherent duality, including heterotopias of deviation, such as prisons, where society effectively places individuals in an alternative reality, and heterotopias of time, such as museums, which house objects from past times in the present (and future).

The discourse around real and imagined spaces is also evident in the work of a number of post-structuralists, notably Baudrillard and his *Simulation and Simulacra* (1981/1994), exploring multiple layers of copy, pretence and simulation in contemporary cultural and media referencing, moving cumulatively toward an expression as simulacra, of the *hyperreal* (Baudrillard 1981/1994). Baudrillard presents three levels of simulacra, attributing each to a particular historical period: the first order, attributed to the pre-modern period, with unique, real and 'irreproducible' objects and situations; the second order of modernity, the Industrial Revolution and mass-reproduction, and the third order of late-stage capitalism, in which the distinction between reality and representation disappears and originality has no meaning.

Foucault's influence is evident too in the work of Edward Soja, whose *Thirdspace: Journeys to Los Angeles and Other Real-and-Imagined Places* (1986) draws on the spatial trialectics of both Foucault's concept of heterotopia, and Lefebvre's *Production of Space* (1974), in which Lefebvre proposes that space is a social product in which historical and current meaning is produced through a three-part relationship between everyday practices and perceptions, or perceived space (*le perçu*), representations or theories of space, or conceived space (*le conçu*) and the spatial imaginary of the time, or lived space (*le vécu*). Soja synthesises Foucault and Lefebvre with other major influences including Homi K Bhabha's 'Third Space Theory', in which 'all forms of culture are continually in a process of hybridity', that 'give rise to something different, something new and unrecognizable' (Bhabha 1994) to introduce the concept of 'thirdspace'. Soja describes thirdspace as 'an-Other way of understanding and acting to change the spatiality of human life, a distinct mode of critical spatial awareness that is appropriate to the new scope and significance being brought about in the rebalanced trialectics of spatiality–historicality–sociality' (Soja 1996). For Soja, thirdspace is 'the space where all places are capable of being seen from every angle, each standing clear; but also, a secret and conjectured object, filled with illusions and allusions, a space that is common to all of us yet never able to be completely seen and understood' (Soja 1996). It is an 'unimaginable universe' in which 'everything comes together… subjectivity and objectivity, the abstract and the concrete, the real and the imagined, the knowable and the unimaginable, the repetitive and the differential, structure and agency, mind and body, consciousness and the unconscious, the disciplined and the transdisciplinary, everyday life and unending history' (Soja 1996), and which can be reached and understood through the process of 'thirding', producing 'a cumulative trialectic that is radically open to additional otherness, to a continuing expansion of spatial knowledge' (Soja 1996).

3.3 The Third Way

This search for a third space is buried deep within the social psyche. From top, middle and bottom, to left, right and centre, to scoring a hat-trick and 'Ready, Steady, Go', the inclination toward the tripartite is evident in so much of our innate organisational patterning. The 'Rule of Three' is a common rhetorical device, designed to present the extremes of an argument and apply the logic of the middle. The same framing lies behind the enduring appeal of so-called 'Third Way' thinking, an ideology with a deep and extensive history, but which is mainly associated in contemporary usage with the mid-1990s work of Anthony Giddens. Positioned in what Giddens describes as the 'radical centre' (Giddens 1991), 'The Third Way' tries to find that sweet spot in between left and right, capitalism and socialism, local and global.

Just as Giddens' original work explored the relationship between the market and state, so Mazzucato continues to explore that relationship, making the case for the state as shaping and creating new markets, arguing that far from being staid and boring, the public sector takes the risk in funding new research for innovation, while the rewards are privatised. Mazzucato makes a 'quality, not quantity' argument for state intervention, asserting that the key question is not its size, but the extent to which it has the capacity and capability to drive an innovation-led, inclusive and sustainable economy through 'symbiotic (not parasitic) public–private partnerships' (Mazzucato 2017).

The fundamental problem with 'Third Way' thinking is that the dichotomies it seeks to synthesise are false. As Mazzucato's work demonstrates, there is a long and well-established interrelationship between the state and the market, albeit of changeable quality across the years. For far too long, the old lie of a separate economy and society has prevailed, and with it the futility of 'Third Way' interventions. The charity model is the stand-out example here. Billions are reinvested back in society by the already tax-paying worker bees in an attempt to rebalance the inequalities and injustices of greed, state failure and extraction. The ironies of this approach are numerous and self-evident. Homelessness charities chaired by property developers. Billionaires donating tiny percentages to the COVID-19 effort. Tax-free celebrities performing on TV telethons.

The economy/society dichotomy is further enforced by the academy and its continued insistence on a distinction between 'the humanities' and 'the sciences'. But economics is a social science. As 'the great pause' has proven, when society stops, the economy stops. Why? Because they are the same thing. Still, the distinction is validated and nowhere more so than within the discipline of economics itself, which continues to assert the neoclassical paradigm over heterodox models. As Steve Keen observes, economics is fairly unique in the sciences in the way it which an approach can be proven as ineffective but continue to be applied at scale. Global crises result only in 'minor modifications…to the core neoclassical paradigm, but fundamental aspects of it remain sacrosanct' (Keen 2020).

The continued tension between neoclassical and heterodox models of economic study, and the related persistence of separating 'the economic' and 'the social', has contributed in recent years to the emergence of several more middle-ground paradigms, in which traditionally social and traditionally economic terminology is simply compounded, creating—through considerable artifice—approaches such as 'inclusive growth'. The world is tentatively exploring 'wellbeing' measures, but only as *additions* to GDP. Prostitution, gambling and illegal drugs continue to be included within GDP calculations of so-called 'productivity'.

Throughout the COVID-19 lockdowns, there has been a plethora of Zoom conferences dedicated to rethinking, reworking, retweaking, rejigging capitalism, to 'doing capitalism differently'. The economic system is stuck in this language of capital and growth, even when the world is choking on it. Our structures, systems and apparatus are designed to support the pursuit of this 'growth at all costs' framework so that even our most radical and progressive models are required to measure and report on jobs, skills, business growth and return on investment measures. Social value is monetised. As a result, the new economy can feel a lot like the old economy, and the call to 'Build Back Better' can feel a lot like building back more of the same.

The calls to return to normal envisage the return of the workers to our worker boxes, building for the benefit of shareholders like economic Stockholm syndrome. Creatures of habit, the irresistible pull is to find safety and security in reverting to what we know and doing what has always been done. The US heads back to Biden when it could have had a Bernie. The UK shuts its eyes to Corbyn as the Boris bus continues, and the UK Labour Party finds itself under the leadership of Starmer, as somewhere a portrait of Tony Blair grows older in an attic.

3.4 It's the Economy, Stupid

Blair's pursuit of 'Third Way' policies in the UK ran alongside the same approach in the US, courtesy of the Clinton administration. During the campaign for Clinton's first presidential term in 1992, his campaign strategist James Carville displayed a sign in the Little Rock headquarters which featured three bulleted reminders to staff, the second of which has since spawned a thousand puns. It read: 'It's the Economy, Stupid'.

Blair, meanwhile, set out his store as 'New Labour', becoming Leader of the Labour Party in 1994 and immediately altering the wording of the party's 'Clause 4', which was changed from a passage expressing the key socialist principle of 'common ownership of the means of production, distribution and exchange' to a new wording themed around 'a community in which power, wealth and opportunity are in the hands of the many, not the few'.

'The Third Way' model was presented as the route to a bounce-back from the early nineties' recession in the US and as a brave new dawn in the UK following eighteen consecutive years of a right-wing government. At its heart, the 'Third Way' advocates for social justice, social cohesion and equal opportunity, but seeks to achieve these goals through the improved distribution of skills and capacities, rather than through wealth redistribution. The approach attempts to find a consensus between what Blair referred to as both 'a modern socialism' and 'a new capitalism'. Roundly critiqued as a neoliberal ideology, and just as unpopular with both laissez-faire capitalists and market socialists, the consensus and compromise which characterised 'Third Way' thinking arguably saw a more positive manifestation in supporting critical cross-party negotiations in Ireland, resulting in the creation of The Good Friday Agreement in 1998. While the agreement brought sharp relief after decades of devastating conflict, the stability of this forced consensus has been tested throughout the resulting power-sharing agreement in Northern Ireland, with long periods during which the Stormont parliament has been unable to sit due to party withdrawal. The fragile peace which exists has been tested further still by the significant pressures of Brexit negotiations.

In 1999, looking once again for a third-route consensus, Blair's administration introduced a middle tier of governance across England, with the introduction of Regional Development Agencies (RDAs). Nine RDAs were established across England, principally concerned with economic development and regeneration, but also supporting those key 'Third Way' drivers of skills and business growth. Coupled with the availability of European funding, this period marked a boom time for the English regions, with significant investment in infrastructure and capital projects in areas that had been previously overlooked, and even neglected, by Westminster. The UK city of Liverpool, famously condemned to 'managed decline' by Thatcher's Home Secretary Lord Howe in his letter of 1981, became a poster-city for European funds, with its city-region of Merseyside benefitting from some £1.6 billion of EU Objective One funding from 1994 to 2007. Neighbouring Manchester also did well from a combination of regional and European funding, gaining a reputation for effective and efficient public–private partnership working in large-scale regeneration and development (characterised as 'The Manchester Model'). This focus on effective partnerships became a national blueprint and a precursor for the formation of the Greater Manchester Combined Authority (GMCA) in 2011, which in turn became a blueprint model for (and driver of) devolved regional governance.

In the summer of 2007, PM Blair handed the UK keys over to PM Brown, just ahead of the financial crash of 2008 and the subsequent deep global recession which marked the following years. In the aftermath of the crash, Brown's government 'bailed out' the banks to the tune of some £500 billion in loans and guarantees, with the G20 also agreeing to simultaneous bank bailouts and austerity measures, in what Yanis Varoufakis calls 'socialism for the banks and austerity for everyone else' (Varoufakis 2020).

3.5 A Fourth Way for 4.0

'A Fourth Way' proposes that instead of 'Building Back Better', we move onward and upward, advancing to and through the 4.0 age by adopting a holistic organisational framework which encourages and fosters collaboration, contribution and collective progress toward shared goals.

'A Fourth Way' recognises 4.0 as an innovation age, realising the 'smart, green golden age' of combined human and technological potential, envisaged as the next post-crisis enlightenment by Carlota Perez (Perez 2016). Underpinned by the need for individual and collective action in response to the challenges of the COVID-19 pandemic, 'A Fourth Way' embraces the current zeitgeist by foregrounding human contribution to innovation as the principal characteristic of the Fourth Industrial Revolution and the 4.0 age. This explicit recognition of human contribution and adoption of a holistic perspective allows for a broader understanding of innovation as not simply a fixed, tangible *product*, a 'thing' which exists in 'innovation districts' and which can be manufactured in labs, developed, commercialised and sold (and which pitches universities, cities and countries against each other in a 'competitive' innovation race), but as a dynamic and networked *process*, a rich and multi-faceted human experience that embraces people as innovators and encourages human creativity, enterprise, endeavour, discourse and dialectical interplay.

Against current and pressing sustainability imperatives, new economic models which seek to express value in terms of human contribution, and which are based on collaborative rather than competitive principles are coming to the fore. Work by Mazzucato (2017, 2021), for example, has brought forward the idea of 'mission-oriented' economies and strategies, moving away from the notion of siloed sectors and individual corporates competing for market share and advocating instead for collective action in tackling social challenges and working toward shared economic goals. 'A Fourth Way' proposes contribution and collaboration as key features of the 4.0 innovation age, moving away from organisational models based on extraction, productivity and endless (spatial) growth. Instead, 'A Fourth Way' proposes an onward and upward, progressive model of growth through a collective investment and accumulation of time. In this model, productivity is reframed as contribution. Time, widely regarded as 'The Fourth Dimension', is prioritised as the focal point of 'A Fourth Way', representing both our global mission and the key metric of shared progress.

3.6 Summary: Change Versus More of the Same

Despite not getting so much attention, the other two bullet points on James Carville's aide memoire for the Clinton campaign back in 1992 have proven to be prescient: 'Don't forget about healthcare', though arguably everybody did, and 'Change vs. more of the same'.

It is notoriously difficult to translate ideas and new economic thinking into policy in the current landscape, and harder still to translate again into practice. The structures, systems and strategies which have successfully sustained (and in some cases been created to promote) 'Third Way' and neoliberal thinking are no longer fit for purpose.

The middle ground, although it feels comfortable and, compared to the extremes, may even seem progressive, is the chasm in which we find a whole range of middlemen; consultancies, place-makers, charities and the media among them, where the direct line from A to B disappears down the whole C. Here too lives capitalism's last stand. Inclusive growth, green growth and clean growth are all examples of capitalism with a conscience, as art-washing, green-washing and well-washing facilitate its rejigging, reimagining and 'great reset'. In this third space consensus, we find progressive ideas constrained, watered down or—worse—capitalised. A number of models propose concepts such as natural capital, in which natural assets are accounted for in capital terms. While a greener form of capitalism may appear progressive, it is nevertheless alarming to note the recent trend for issuing shares in tree stocks.

The middle ground presents itself as consensus in a world of polarities, but it is littered with hypocrisy and conscience wringing. Devolution gives with one hand while austerity takes with the other, billions is sunk into a Victorian-era charity model which serves only to alleviate immediate challenges as opposed to generating solutions, and the UK government's current push to 'level up' so-called 'left-behind' communities comes after ten full years of levelling those same communities out. In practice, the pursuit of a middle —a centre—follows post-structuralist theory by also creating peripheries and margins, which can result in turn in creating surplus and marginalisation. In a specific example of the limitations of 'Third Way' approaches, Greater Manchester, home to the celebrated 'Manchester Model' of regeneration founded on hyper-development, agglomeration and public–private partnership, has in recent years faced a severe crisis of homelessness. A 2020 survey by UK homelessness charity Shelter found that 8000 citizens across Greater Manchester were experiencing homelessness and 80,000 more were waiting for housing allocations on its applications list for social housing (BBC News 2020).

Greater Manchester is not alone in experiencing homelessness as a consequence of hyper-development. Arguably, Manchester's development model has followed the London blueprint and has in turn been followed by other metropolitan cities such as Liverpool, all with similar results. Instead of learning from the consequences of pursuing this approach in other cities, the emergence of homelessness as a crisis has either been ignored or regarded as collateral damage. So much attention has been paid to the changes happening across urban skylines that dogged pursuit of development at all costs has remained ignorant to the changes happening in urban doorways. Despite significant efforts by charities, faith groups and civic leaders, including GM Mayor Andy Burnham donating a percentage of his monthly salary to a Mayoral charity established to support efforts to reduce homelessness and rough sleeping, progress remains slow. The Mayoral charity is chaired by a prominent local property developer. A leading homelessness charity in Manchester is housed in office space donated by another leading property development company. A third property developer has recently launched a city-wide initiative to end homelessness. For-profit property development continues, at pace and scale.

The 'Third Way' approach offers only short-term solutions, and only while the terms of the consensus remain acceptable to still-polarised parties. Its short-termism has been roundly demonstrated by the inglorious 2008 economic crash which followed the glorious spending of the Blair/Clinton years. More recently, the spectre—and ongoing spectacle—of Brexit has once again riled tensions in Ireland. The Republic of Ireland remains in Europe and attempts as part of the negotiations to determine a position for a border between Europe and the UK have served to alert parties on both sides to the fragility of the terms agreed in the Good Friday Agreement which, according to commentator Patrick Kielty, has been revealed as an accord based only on 'a slight of hand' (Kielty 2020).

After a decade of austerity and a global pandemic, it will take more than a return to 'Third Way' neoliberalism to rebalance the books. 'A Fourth Way' proposes adoption of holistic principles, based on a fourth space perspective and coupled with a deep and comprehensive understanding of both place and time. Underpinning panonomics, which in turn is envisaged as a holistic organisational model able to meet the universal needs of the pandemic, 'A Fourth Way' is the key to our progress through the 4.0

age, to achieving sustainability goals and a rallying call for change, versus more of the same.

References

BBC News (2020) https://www.bbc.co.uk/news/uk-england-manchester-55208787. Accessed 14 December 2020.
Baudrillard, J (1981/1994) Simulacra and Simulation. University of Michigan Press.
Bhabha, HK (1994) The Location of Culture. Routledge: London.
Derrida, J (1972) Structure, Signs and Play in the Discourse of Human Sciences. Baltimore: Johns Hopkins University Press.
Foucault, M (1973) The Order of Things: An Archaeology of the Human Sciences, trans R. Howard. New York: Vintage Press.
Foucault, M (1986) The History of Sexuality, Volume 3: The Care of the Self, trans R. Hurley. New York: Pantheon.
Giddens, A (1991) The Third Way: The Renewal of Social Democracy. London: Wiley.
Granovetter, M (1985) 'Economic Action and Social Structure, the Problem of Embeddedness', American Journal of Sociology Volume 91, Issue 3. Chicago. University of Chicago Press.
Heidegger, M (1927/2019) Being and Time, trans. Macquarrie, R, and Robinson, ES. Connecticut: Martino Fine Books.
Keen, S (2020) https://www.patreon.com/posts/introduction-to-43848097. Accessed 11 December 2020.
Kielty, P (2020) The Good Friday Agreement. Accessed 4 July 2021.
Lacan, J (1955) The Seminar. Book II. The Ego in Freud's Theory and in the Technique of Psychoanalysis trans. Sylvania Tomaselli. Cambridge: Cambridge University Press.
Lefebvre, H (1992) Rhythmanalysis: Space, Time and Everyday Life. London: Bloomsbury.
Mazzucato, M (2017) The Entrepreneurial State. London: Penguin.
Mazzucato, M (2021) Mission Economy. London: Penguin.
Perez, C (2016) Capitalism, Technology and a Green Global Golden Age. London: IIPP.
Saussure, F de (1916/1983) ed. Harris, R. Course in General Linguistics. London: Bloomsbury.
Soja, E (1996) Thirdspace: Journeys to Los Angeles and Other Real-and-Imagined Places. Oxford: Blackwell.
Varoufakis, Y (2020) Another Now: Dispatches from an Alternative Present. Bodley Head.

CHAPTER 4

Mission: Time—'The Why'

Abstract Time—the fourth dimension—is the key focal point and metric in the panonomic model. The COVID-19 pandemic and associated lockdowns have left us with a vastly distorted sense of time. As we make our way through, and hopefully emerge from, the pandemic, we are immediately faced with the time-critical challenges presented by climate collapse. Considering our deep interrelationship with time and building on Mazzucato's work around mission-oriented economies, Hawking's seminal concept of 'Imaginary Time', Heidegger's interplay of time and care, and the three primary concepts of time used in orthodox economics (historical, logical and intemporal), here we introduce a fourth concept of transcendental time, envisaged as an onward movement toward the future in an upward spiral motion. Contextualising panonomics within a future conceived of as a perpetual series of 'Future Nows', the accumulation of time is proposed as our principal collective mission and the key measurement of our shared and forward progress.

Keywords Time · Fourth dimension · Care · Upward spiral · Future Now

C. Devaney, *Panonomics*,
https://doi.org/10.1007/978-3-030-87509-1_4

4.1 Introduction: Mission—Time

Tick, tock. From the very second that we are born, time, the great healer, becomes an ever-present in our lives; themselves just extended passages of time. Tick, tock, tick, tock.

Bleary-eyed and discombobulated, checking the time is for many the first action, and point of grounding, in the daily routine. As we make our way with a similar bleary-eyed discombobulation through the stages of a global pandemic, there is a similar sense of the need to stop, to regroup and to ground ourselves to a moment. A collective checking of the time.

The pandemic has brought death and grief, pain, illness, discomfort and loss, in huge and devastating numbers. Robbing us of lives, of time with our loved ones and necessitating a series of 'lockdowns', the pandemic has thrown the world order into disarray. With no work to go to, no clock to watch, nowhere to go and no rush to get there, the whole notion and experience of time has been subject to what commentators have called the 'Anthropause' (Rutz et al. 2020). Fitting, then, that the standout teenage craze emerging from the lockdowns has been an online platform for self-edited videos called 'TikTok'. Limited to fifteen seconds per upload, the self-edited videos allow the user to speed up or slow down material with a 'warp' feature; a feature which, at times has felt to have crossed the 'fourth wall' to warp our world in real time.

Turning the 'TikTok' camera on ourselves in this unprecedented pause to reflect, we find a contemporary concept of time that has been almost suffocated by its commodification. Hours are measured in a monetary rate and the '9–5' job has made way for the precariat, the minimum wage, the living wage and, in the starkest dereliction of time, the advent of zero hours contracts. Time is measured in money, and it has become so tethered to money that it is hard to extricate it from its grasp. In its most grotesque form, economies measured in productivity ascribe a value to human life in terms of what that life can produce. GDP does not have a moral code. It includes 'product' generated through prostitution, the arms trade and illegal drugs—three established pillars in the dark world of trafficking. This difficult fact is routinely ignored by advocates for productivity as a measure of our individual and collective progress and economic success. The notion of 'human capital' maintains a veneer of respectability, but there is a damascene moment when that notion is extended to the well-used economic accounting phrase of 'human capital stock'.

Unsurprisingly, there is a particular jarring when productivity meets health. Care takes time. To meet efficiency targets, appointment times with GPs, district nurses and home carers are time-limited, hospital beds are prioritised over the patients inside them and, ultimately, the value of keeping a person alive is balanced against the associated cost. Meanwhile, UK economic strategy seeks to fill the so-called 'productivity gap', a term used to describe the extent to which the GDP of the North of England lags behind as compared to the South (and particularly London, at its epicentre). Strategy after strategy has been developed to figure out how this gap might be filled; the dominant theory relating to the relatively poor health outcomes of the Northern workforce. Improving health by x%, we are told, will close the productivity gap by x%. At the core of that thinking is the idea is that the healthier we are, the more we can produce. A little like dairy cows.

Just like those dairy cows, it turns out that over-productivity might not be so good for our health. Prefaced by a long overdue destigmatising of mental health issues, alongside an increased awareness of the threat and grim realities of mental burnout, the world of economics has increasingly embraced the concept of wellbeing, with Iceland, Scotland, Germany and New Zealand taking the lead in developing 'wellbeing economies' (see Hoekstra et al. 2020). While this feels like progress, in each current case the approach is to promote the value of 'wellbeing' alongside GDP, demonstrating an unstable consensus and a middle-ground approach characteristic of the neoliberal 'Third Way'.

Admittedly, it would be difficult for any country to unilaterally declare the end of GDP, despite the swathes of work that expose the shaky ground on which it is built. At a city-level, Amsterdam has been the first to strike out from the GDP paradox, adopting Kate Raworth's *Doughnut Economics* (2017) model and its optimal parameters for growth in meeting social and planetary needs. In the UK, the latest approach to gain traction is 'Community Wealth Building' (Guinan et al. 2020), an approach which seeks to minimise extraction from local economies (through, for example, property rents) and instead to generate local benefits through reinvestment in the local economy and community ownership models. Expressed in the present continuous verb form—that is, being *in the process of* building, it is arguably far more palatable to the established status quo than the idea of 'Community Wealth' itself.

Both of these emerging models apply spatial boundaries. Community Wealth Building is a place-based approach and focusses on bordered communities of place. Raworth's model invites us to imagine a shape and form for the economy as a series of 'sweet spots', doughnut-like interconnected rings which create an optimal space between a conceptual 'social floor' and 'planetary ceiling', hosting a compromise between human needs and the limits of planetary resources (Raworth 2017).

Deconstructing the base formula of the capital model—the value of space over time, panonomics proposes that we shift away from spatially focussed concepts and toward the other element within that base formula—time, the fourth dimension. While investment in space is notoriously speculative and inherently competitive thanks to its limited availability as a finite resource, investment in time brings a paradoxical certainty with its uncertainty. The risk of investment in space increases over time, with all the unknown variables that that brings, but investment in time as an infinite resource—the only alternative being that it is not infinite, in which case it's game over anyway—effectively eliminates that risk. Rather than proposing degrowth as a way in which to limit our extraction from the planet's increasingly limited spatial resource, panonomics proposes that our shared mission and the focus of our primary organisational model should be our collective growth toward and investment in and of time. The great constant offers a future without boundaries, and a certainty in the uncertainty of the infinite.

4.2 Time: The Fourth Dimension

Like space, time has been the subject of a constant literary, cultural, scientific and philosophical investigation. The 'wheel of time' concept, present in a number of religions including Hinduism and Buddhism, emerged in ancient Indian thinking, such as the *Veda* texts dating from approximately 2000BC, which assert that the universe goes through repeated cycles of creation, destruction and rebirth. In Greek mythology, Khronos was venerated as the personification of time and often represented as an aged man (adopted in later folklore as 'Old Father Time'). The prominent belief in Ancient Greek philosophy was that time was conceptual, unreal and illusionary, respectively, explored by Antiphon, Parminedes and Zeno (the latter through his 'Paradoxes'), although a number of contemporaries also considered 'real' and material time, such as Heraclitus' description of time as 'the essence of reality'. Plato believed in creationism and regarded time as a creation from God (the basis too for St. Augustine's later descriptions of time and 'divine eternity') but also put forward the idea of time as a movement between celestial bodies. Plato's student Artistotle believed in infinite time, (a non-creationist position), setting time out in the linear past-present-future and regarded time as a quantified ('numbered') measurement of change, both of which are familiar in modern Western understanding (see Whitrow 1972).

Two schools of thought dominated much of the scientific exploration of time in early modern philosophy, namely Newton's 'absolute time' and 'relational time' advocated by Kant and others. Newton asserted that time is part of the fundamental structure of the universe, and that it can best be looked on as a dimension in which events occur in sequence (leading, in later scientific study, and common vernacular, time to be described as 'the fourth dimension'). In Newton's theory, time is an entity in its own right and exists independently of any perceiver, progresses at a consistent pace throughout the universe, is imperceptible, and can only be understood mathematically. Relational time presents time as an abstract, which ceases to have any meaning or manifest unless there are objects with which it can interact or relate. In *Critique of Pure Reason* (1781), Immanuel Kant describes both space and time as 'a priori' notions which do not have structural form, but which are necessary perceptions for human comprehension of experience. Kant's chief assertion is that time while empirically real (that is, not illusionary) 'transcendentally ideal' (Kant 1781/1999).

In his magnum opus *Being and Time* (1927), Martin Heidegger sets out on what he calls the 'destruction' of philosophical tradition, rejecting in its course both the linear Aristotelian model of time, which he describes as 'vulgar' and the notion of a 'divine infinity' as set out by St. Augustine. Instead, Heidegger's work is set firmly in the context of the existential analytic of *Dasein*, a fusion of the subject (being) and the object (world), intended to embody a "living being" through their activity of 'being there' and 'being in the world' (Horrigan Kelly et al. 2016). Critchley (2009) notes that 'the basic idea of *Being and Time* is extremely simple: being is time. That is, what it means for a human being to be is to exist temporally in the stretch between birth and death. Being is time and time is finite, it comes to an end with our death', and asserts a directionality of time as implicit in *Dasein*, which he translates as 'being-towards-death' (Critchley 2009). While this notion may sound morbid to the contemporary ear, Heidegger in effect removes any implicit morbidity with his assertion that 'higher than actuality stands possibility' (Heidegger 1927/2019) advocating in essence not for a passive awaiting of death, but for a positive acceptance of mortality in order to liberate possibility.

Heidegger presents three *ecstaces* of time: the concept of *Gewesenheit* or 'having-been-ness' (Critchley 2009) to describe the 'emotional baggage' of the past, *Augenblick* or 'the glance of the eye' (also used in Lutheran theology) to describe the present and, in typical style, makes a linguistic play between 'the future' (*zukunft*) and to come toward (*zukommen*). Being is not confined to the present but always projects to the future.

Time is a well-established factor in mainstream economics and primarily used in relation to exploring sequential behaviours of capital investments over time, as in Böhm-Bawerk's theory of 'time preference', dating from the late 1800s, Samuelson's theory of 'time-discounting' in the 1930s, Koopman's addition of 'impatience' in the 1960s, and more recently in behavioural economics, particularly in work relating to the role of human emotions and preferences in 'time use' (such as Kahneman and Krueger's U-index 2006). There are three main classifications of time used in economic analysis: logical, historical and intertemporal (Bausor and Shackle 1982). Bausor and Shackle (1982) describe these classifications in terms of their application to points A and B. *Logical* time is time-related to causality between point A and point B, where both points are impacted by an event or events (or indeed by each other). *Historical* time, with which we are more familiar in everyday life, puts points A and B in order of chronological sequence. *Intertemporal* time refers to what something might look or behave like at point B compared to point A, primarily applied in economics to behaviours and choices in relation to investments, including of investment of time itself (Bausor and Shackle 1982).

In his seminal work *A Brief History of Time* (1988), Stephen Hawking introduces the concept of 'imaginary time', a mathematical deceit of sorts which removes singular events like 'The Big Bang' from the past-present-future horizontal sequencing of 'real time' and instead introduces the prospect of a vertical time horizon hosting multiple and simultaneous events, which can happen at any point between the two axes - *imaginary time*. By removing the boundaries of 'real time', themselves occurring as singularities along a horizontal axis (a particular year, for example), Hawking also disrupts the equation of spacetime so that spatial boundaries are also removed, presenting the possibility of an infinite universe.

4.3 Time as Care, Community and Citizenship

In *Being and Time*, Heidegger uses three forms of expression rooted in the German word '*sorge*' or 'care'. *Sorge* represents concern for itself. It is reflective and, as such, concerned with the past. *Besorgen* represents action, the immediate provision of care, and relates to the present. *Fursorge* represents being concerned for others and relates to prevention or intervention (such as welfare). It relates to the future and 'leaps ahead of the other' to give *sorge* back to him/her (Dahlstrom 2013). 'Temporality', Heidegger writes 'reveals itself to be the sense of authentic care' (Heidegger 1927/2019).

In a present in which we are recovering from a global pandemic (and an associated widespread 'crisis of care') and with an increasing awareness of the impending threat of climate collapse, it is small wonder perhaps that both 'care' and 'time' feature large in current and emerging economic models and systems. Hillary Cottam's 2018 book *Radical Help* proposes a new model of social welfare provision (envisaged as a 'fit for purpose' successor to the welfare state) which is based on human relationships, social connections and collective capacity, foregrounding care as 'the compost within which everything else takes root' (Cottam 2018). In *The Good Ancestor* (2020), Roman Krznaric calls for a 'deep time humility' and prioritising our future descendants over the 'pathological short-termism' of our current political cycles, short-term consumerist mores and growth-fixated economic model. 'Promoting greater intergenerational justice', Krznaric writes, 'guided by the transcendent goal of creating a world in which the needs of future generations can be met with the resources on our finite planet—"one-planet thriving"—should be a major goal of anyone aspiring to become a good ancestor. If people just don't care, we're doomed' (Krznaric 2020).

Reinforced by the wealth of community spirit and connection that has emerged during the pandemic and its necessary adaptations and 'lockdowns', many emerging models are founded on community building and collective action (as opposed to competition). 'Community Wealth Building', a term first used by The Democracy Collaborative in the US in relation to its work with people and communities in Cleveland, is the latest economic model (following 'inclusive growth') to gain prominence in the UK. The Centre for Local Economic Strategies (CLES) has facilitated much of the work in the UK. In '*Owning the Future. After Covid-19: A New Era of Community Wealth Building*' (Guinan et al. 2020), CLES identifies five pillars of the Community Wealth Building approach: financial flows, land and property use, local spending and progressive workforce practices, all redirected toward the fifth pillar, 'building the generative economy', characterised as 'locking wealth into place' (Guinan et al. 2020).

Elinor Ostrom's work around polycentricity (2010) sets out her thinking on those aspects of economy that 'do not fit into a dichotomous world of "the market" and "the state"' (Ostrom 2010). Famously advocating for locality, diversity and autonomy in communities and for community self-governance of shared assets or resources as 'the commons', Ostrom's work is once again finding resonance in contemporary economic theory and practice. A similar call to acknowledge community alongside marker and state features in the work of former International Monetary Fund Chief Raghuram Rajan, who argues for the importance of community in *The Third Pillar* (2019) as the 'third pillar' of the title.

The New Citizenship Project (NCP) notes a 'post-COVID' emergence not only of community and collectivism, but of collective community activism as a current expression of what it calls 'The Citizen Shift' (NCP 2015), a three-stage movement in self-identification, both individually and as the collective conscious, from *subjects* to *consumers* to *citizens*. This burst of citizenship is observable too in the rise of new civic movements across the world. The Black Lives Matter movement, the #metoo movement, democratic protests in Hong Kong and school strikes in protest of climate change have all come forward to show solidarity and to demand and secure justice, action and change.

4.4 Caring for Time: An Upward Spiral

In *Marx, Capital and the Madness of Economic Reason* (2017), David Harvey describes the capitalist phenomenon of globalisation as 'the annihilation of space over time' (Harvey 2017). He notes a particular paradox to be found in 'fixed capital' which, Harvey says, 'engages the labour of future use. Embedded in the land, it must be used in situ if it is to be redeemed over time. The very form of flow designed to liberate capital therefore ends up directing the flow back into that space' (Harvey 2017). Harvey describes three typologies of spatiotemporal value flows: linear, cyclical and capital, characterising the last of these as 'the downward spiral of globalisation' and describing it as 'representing the capital flow of anti-value based on the accumulation of debt as a claim on future labour' (Harvey 2017).

Harvey's terminology and choice of language reflect the disregard and carelessness with which the planet's spatial resources have been brutalised by the capitalist economy. Its focus on extraction is apparent too in the well-established 'three-sector model' (Fisher 1939; Fourastié 1949), which puts forward a model of economic transformation based on a shift from a primary economy, that is based principally on agriculture and the extraction of resources, to a secondary economy, that is based principally on industry and manufacture, to a tertiary economy, that is based principally on provision of services. The model was extended in the last twentieth century (Kenessey 1987; Selstad 1990) to include a quaternary sector, that is based principally on knowledge and human capacity.

Rejecting the original model's framing in extraction, panonomics extends the identified characteristics of the quaternary sector to propose a model based instead on the contribution of knowledge and capacity. In *Mission Economy*, Mariana Mazzucato asserts that 'Economic growth has not only a rate but also a direction' (Mazzucato 2021). Panonomics, in direct oppose to the 'downward spiral' of globalisation identified by Harvey (2017), and responding to Krznaric's call for care and a 'deep time humility' (Krznaric 2020), proposes a collective and progressive growth, moving in an 'upward spiral' flow. The spiral forms a conical shape, representing the collection and galvanising of place-driven strengths at its base, gathering momentum to move onward and upward—through collective investment of care and contribution—toward the shared mission of time.

4.5 Transcendental Time and a Future Now

Panonomics is rooted in this deep understanding of time and embedded in the cultural heritage of place. There is an inherent interrelationship between heritage and time, as captured by the RSA's definition of heritage as 'anything inherited from the past that helps us, collectively or individually, to understand the present, and create a (better) future' (RSA 2017) and UNESCO's 2003 definition of 'intangible cultural heritage as "traditions or living expressions inherited from our ancestors and passed on to our descendants" (UNESCO 2003).

The panonomic model reflects both the flow and motility of time by incorporating both a (cyclical) dynamism and a directionality (in an upward spiral motion). Echoing Kant's description of time as 'transcendentally ideal', panonomics introduces the concept of 'transcendental time', envisaged as incorporating and transcending the established triad of historical, chronological and intertemporal time (Bausor and Shackle 1982). Adopting this fourth layer, a four-dimensional understanding of time and accepting its ability to transcend the limitations of temporal boundaries allows us to conceive of an ability to accumulate 'chunks of time' and to put ourselves in the future, now. Conceiving of our actions not just as having implications for a conceptual future, but for a real 'Future Now', panonomics is a call not just for limiting human impact on the planet, but for positive contribution through pro-actively investing our time and resources in making more time.

Panonomics envisages our continued progress as an ad infinitum accumulation of time, advancing in perpetual motion toward a successive series of 'Future Nows', in which each now is another now's future.

4.6 Summary: Making Time

Time, gentlemen please.

Alcohol is not best known for boosting productivity, but it is a huge earner for the UK Treasury, generating an annual £44bn in direct sales and £10bn in tax revenues. Off licences, naturally, have been designated as 'essential shops' in successive national/UK lockdowns.

The concept of time has become unrecognisably distorted during those lockdowns, due in no small part to the monetary value which is ascribed to time through the labour market—and the pandemic's sharp removal of that market.

'Time is money', so the saying goes. We spend time, save time, invest time and make time. Debt is measured in years. We commit to '5-year' loans and '25-year' mortgages. Paper money is not valuable because of the paper from which it is made. Its value comes from the time we invest in exchange for its reward. We 'earn a living'—in essence, earning a right to more time. Decisions are made as to the value of each person's time, with the increase in precariat jobs setting this out in stark per hour or, worse, zero-hour terms. There is not only a minimum wage—a minimum value of a person's labour, expressed in time—but its successor the living wage, and its successor the real living wage. As we have seen with 'affordable housing', since superseded by 'genuinely affordable homes', the addition of modifiers to already subjective terms like affordable, liveable and basic, only adds further subjectivity and confusion.

Lockdown has forced us to extract our concept of time from its ascribed monetary value and to recalibrate. In many of the new narratives, time takes precedence over space. The last year has seen the advent of '15-minute cities' as restrictions on travel amplify the need for locally available services and resources (and a more leisurely 20 minutes proposed in the Scottish national planning framework). Paris is leading the way on this narrative, with Mayor Anne Hidalgo setting out plans to ensure that every resident is able to fulfil their daily activities and meet necessities within a 15-minute walk or cycle. While the 15-minute aspect itself is of interest from a fairly radical planning perspective, it is in fact the time saved around the 15 minutes that creates the human interest. What could you be doing on the Left Bank with the notional hour of time *saved*, instead of elbowing your way through the Paris Metro on a rush-hour commute?

Just as those Metro commuters are saving time, panonomics proposes that we can work collectively to invest our time and contribution in saving time and in making more time. The model sets time—and its integral links to survival and sustainability—as the primary global mission, and proposes that, to meet the ongoing challenges of the pandemic and our shared sustainability goals, all of our human innovation capacity, skills and knowledge should be focussed intensely on the accumulation—the making—of more time. Millions of hours saved on the Left Bank could have a dramatic effect in making time for our species and for the planet, easing our collective long-term commute toward the Future Now.

References

Bausor, R and Shackle, GLS (1982) Time and the Structure of Economic Analysis. Oxford: Taylor and Francis.

Cottam, H (2018) Radical Help. London: Virago.

Critchley, M (2009) Being and Time: Why Heidegger Matters. Accessed 4 July 2021.

Dahlstrom, DO (2013) The Heidegger Dictionary. London: Bloomsbury.

Fisher, AGB (1939) Production, Primary, Secondary and Tertiary. London: Economic Record.

Fourastié, J (1949) *Le grand espoir du XXe siècle: Progrès technique, progrès économique, progrès social* (in French). Paris: Presses universitaires de France.

Guinan, J, Mcinroy, N, Liebowitz, J, and Mckinley, S (2020) Owning the Future: After Covid-19, A New Era of Community Wealth Building. Manchester: CLES.

Harvey, D (2017) Marx, Capital and the Madness of Economic Reason. London: Profile.

Hawking, S (1988) A Brief History of Time: From the Big Bang to Black Holes. London: Penguin.

Heidegger, M (1927/2019) Being and Time, trans. Macquarrie, R, Robinson, ES. CT: Martino Fine Books.

Hoekstra, R et al. (2020) 'Measuring the Wellbeing Economy: How to Go Beyond-GDP', Wellbeing Economy Alliance.

Horrigan Kelly, M, Millar, M, and Dowling, M (2016) Understanding the Key Tenets of Heidegger's Philosophy for Interpretive Phenomenological Research. London: Sage.

Kahneman, D and Krueger, AB (2006) 'Developments in the Measurement of Subjective Well-Being', Journal of Economic Perspectives.

Kant, I (1781/1999) Critique of Pure Reason, ed. Allen, W, Guyer, P. Cambridge: Cambridge University Press.

Krznaric, R (2020) The Good Ancestor. London: Penguin.

Mazzucato, M (2021) Mission Economy. London: Penguin.

New Citizenship Project (2020) https://medium.com/new-citizenship-project/subject-consumer-or-citizen-three-post-covid-futures-8c3cc469a984. Accessed 12 December 2020.

Ostrom, Elinor (2010) 'Beyond Markets and States: Polycentric Governance of Complex Economic Systems', The American Economic Review. www.jstor.org/stable/27871226. Accessed 13 December 2020.

Rajan, R (2019) The Third Pillar. London: William Collins.

Raworth, K (2017) Doughnut Economics. London: Random House.

RSA (2017) Heritage, Identity and Place. London: The Royal Society of Arts.

Rutz C, Loretto MC, Bates AE, Davidson SC, Duarte CM, Jetz W, et al. (September 2020). "COVID-19 Lockdown Allows Researchers to Quantify the Effects of Human Activity on Wildlife." Accessed 4 July 2021.

UNESCO (2003) What Is Cultural Heritage? https://ich.unesco.org/en/what-is-intangible-heritage-00003. Accessed 4 July 2021.

Whitrow, GJ (1972) What Is Time? Oxford: Oxford University Press.

CHAPTER 5

A People's Panonomics: 'The Who'

Abstract The panonomic model is founded on a deep and comprehensive understanding of place. Like heritage, which so often finds itself subsumed into a tourism agenda, contemporary iterations of place, and the related practice of placemaking, are rolled into an outward facing 'place marketing'. The result can feel like something which is focussed primarily on people who are not from the place in question, rather than those who are. This dissonance with place is evident in the indistinct, 'place-blind' approaches to innovation development, in which 'bandwagon' sectors such as digital and biotechnology are claimed as specialisms, the social challenges of place are glossed over, and indigenous and tacit knowledge is routinely ignored. Panonomics proposes instead foundation on a holistic and comprehensive 'whole spectrum' expression of place, which embraces all characteristics, aspects and facets of places, and through which the full capacity of the people of a place can contribute toward shared goals. Rejecting GDP as a mono-centric and no longer fit-for-purpose approach to evaluation, panonomics proposes a multi-criteria framework for measuring progress which draws on the unique human experiences of place and which reflects the distinct complexities, interconnectivities and dynamics of particular places, of communities of place, and of people within those communities.

Keywords People · Community · Measurement · Time, · Experience · Complexity

C. Devaney, *Panonomics*,
https://doi.org/10.1007/978-3-030-87509-1_5

5.1 Introduction: Start with People

The strength and power of people and communities, voluntary organisations and locally rooted social enterprises has been re-stated emphatically during the pandemic and lockdowns. In contrast to a crippled private sector and a slow and cumbersome state, these 'creative, frontline responders' (Erika Rushton 2020) have been able to adapt at pace, and to respond with deep local knowledge, foresight and agility. The RSA's portfolio of work on *Heritage, Identity and Place* (2017) concludes that approaches to place should 'Start with People'. Panonomics does just that. The people and communities of place are the drivers in the 'place-driven' model.

Despite this burst of hyper-localism which has sustained local economies during the pandemic and lockdowns, the property development machine rolls on through 'top down' calls to 'Build Back Better'. Masterplans (from the masters) are still a prominent feature in regeneration strategies, with an ever-present invisible hand ready to artificially create place. These orchestrated attempts at placemaking are often accompanied by declarations of a place as an innovation district or a cultural or creative quarter, drawn in marker on maps and spearheaded by consultancies who are hired to engage with the communities of that place as mediators of the message. Place, community and culture have all been instrumentalised in some way in the name of development, and for corporate and commercial interests. Placemaking has become an industry, which comes with global conferences and memberships. It is a far cry from the placemaking of Jan Gehl and his 'human scale' (Gehl 1971).

5.2 Community Development

Like placemaking, 'community development' is another of those compounded terms frequently found in policy where the agent of the verb is obscure—is the community doing the development or being developed? Both the practice and the term are questionable, having evidenced roots in British colonialism and particularly in Kenya and East Africa. In the UK, the term came back into to prominence with the introduction of the 'Community Development Programme' (CDP) under Wilson's Labour Government in 1969, a scheme which continued until the Thatcher Government in 1979, with—unsurprisingly—little more in the way of community development policy in the UK until Blair's tenure as Prime Minister, from 1997.

Under Blair's first term of government and alongside the drive for regional development, new partnerships were forged between local authorities, city-regional public sector 'quango' agencies and private sector developers in the delivery of large-scale urban and suburban regeneration programmes, resulting in significant capital development in cities and towns across the UK. Under the 'New Deal for Communities' (NDC) programme, the Department for Communities and Local Government (DCLG) launched some thirty-nine NDC partnerships across England in 1998/9, but by Blair's second term it was apparent that the New Deal felt very much like the old deal and that the 'boom' being experienced in richer areas across the South of England, and principally manifest in rising house prices, was not being replicated in the post-industrial urban areas across the North of England and the Midlands. This in turn resulted in the introduction of the notorious Housing Market Renewal (HMR) programme and its Pathfinder initiative in 2002, which earmarked nine 'Pathfinder' areas of particularly low demand for intervention, including Manchester/Salford, Merseyside, Newcastle/Gateshead and Birmingham/Sandwell. Envisaged and promoted as a 'neighbourhood improvement' programme, the Pathfinder initiative rolled out in practice as a large-scale programme of clearance and demolition, drawing widespread criticism, protest and challenge as a thinly opaque attempt at social engineering, and none more so than from people living in the already-established communities within the clearance areas.

Despite the addition of three more areas to the Pathfinder initiative in 2005, taking the total to twelve, the HMR programme was ended abruptly by David Cameron's coalition government in March 2011. As predicted by a Joseph Rowntree Foundation review of the programme in 2004, poor planning and its earlier than expected cessation meant that the HMR left a legacy characterised more by demolition than renewal. Thanks in part to its abrupt end, a number of sites were not redeveloped as planned, resulting in large and seemingly ad-hoc grassed over areas being left at demolition sites, many of which can still be observed in former Pathfinder areas today.

The key failure of the HMR programme was that its rollout became solely about the built (or rather, demolished) environment and the market. It forgot about the people. While it is not generally remembered with any great fondness or acclaim, the HMR experience was nevertheless pivotal in the emergence and nature of place, and placemaking, and particularly in ideas around 'community development', notably in underlining the futility of attempts to artificially create communities (and place), and in underscoring the strength of communities and revealing the richness, depth and complexity in how communities are formed and established. Communities revealed themselves to be neither homogenous nor malleable to the demands of the market, with the big take-away being that 'the community' is not a passive entity ready and waiting to be regenerated and developed.

5.3 Communities of Place

Two things happened in the HMR afterglow. First, Cameron's coalition government and its austerity politics made swinging cuts to local authority budgets and, in turn, to front line services, while at the same time coming up with the 'Big Society' campaign, the latter widely critiqued as a vehicle to encourage people and communities to fill the gaps created by the former. In a notable divergence away from the physical interventions of HMR, the programme's stated aims included the creation of more social action, empowerment of communities and opening up public services, but its delivery resulted instead in increased exposure of those services to the private sector. A 2014 audit of the campaign by Civil Exchange is nothing short of damning in its evaluation that it resulted in a significantly weakened charitable and voluntary sector, with only a little uplift in volunteering and negligible in the poorest areas. 'The Big Society has not reached those who need it most' the review concludes, adding that 'We are more divided than before' (Civil Exchange 2015).

And second, communities started doing it for themselves. Approaches based on communities as assets rather than communities of need had already started to emerge, running alongside physical development (including ABCD, or 'Asset Based Community Development'), but there was remained a critical question over agency in how these programmes were delivered in practice. While the theoretical principles of ABCD state that citizens should be agents of development and that control should lie within the community, this iteration of ABCD was delivered in practice by organisations and institutions working with communities. In the UK, it was adopted as an approach by several housing associations and registered social landlords who, through the push on housing-led, physical regeneration programmes like HMR, had become a quasi-public face, a 'front-door' to the community. The notion of 'community empowerment' also came to prominence at this time. Like placemaking, there are questions to be asked about the power dynamics of empowerment, and—critically—the identity of the agent in the verb.

In several cases, the community became its own agent. In 2011, for example, after many long and arduous years of dealing with various local and Government interventions and their cumulative impacts—including the HMR programme—residents in the Granby area of Toxteth in Liverpool, UK formed the Granby Four Streets Community Land Trust (CLT). Directed by a Trustee board of local residents and supported by a mix of charitable funding and philanthropic social investment, the CLT took on ownership of a number of houses and shops in the area, working with Liverpool City Council in the years 2011–2015 on innovative programmes like the homesteading programme (which saw a number of derelict properties sold to local individuals and families for £1 in exchange for redevelopment and a commitment to being resident in the home for five-years plus). Residents have since established a popular and vibrant monthly market. The Granby Winter Garden, an indoor garden and community space, was launched by the CLT in 2019.

5.4 Embeddedness: Cultural Heritage as the Key

As countless Government schemes, including the Community Development Programme of the seventies, the HMR Pathfinder and latterly The Big Society have proven, neither community nor place can be created and installed. Attempts to create place and to somehow inject culture tend to result in anodyne and disconcertingly sterile settings. In sharp contrast, Liverpool's Granby community, for example, has a rich, diverse and organic cultural heritage, founded in and bonded by the place, brought together by families, friendships and fallouts, melded by shared years of memories, victories, horror, heartaches and battles won and lost.

This kind of deeply bonded 'culture of place' cannot be created artificially or to order, but that does not stop schemes from trying. Stephen Pritchard writes extensively about 'artwashing', which he describes as 'how art is used as a gloss for dispossession, displacement and, ultimately, social cleansing' (Pritchard 2017). As ever, our artists are front and centre of the charge for change, but also the most at risk, both from attempts to instrumentalise their work, and from the threat of displacement through neighbourhood gentrification.

Instead, panonomics is envisaged as deeply embedded in the cultural heritage of place, embracing the view expressed by the cultural materialist Raymond Williams that culture is 'the whole of life' (Williams 1958). The depth of this embeddedness within the fabric of place and over a heritage steeped in time is offered as a balancing counterpoint which, by embedding the 'Future Now' within the current and the past, will support resilience, longevity and sustainability into that future now. Reflecting Granovetter's understanding of embeddeness in 'concrete, ongoing social relations' (Granovetter 1985), panonomics presents a dynamic and place-driven model which is embedded in the concrete, ongoing *cultural* relations of place.

5.5 Measuring in the Key of Life

This holistic understanding of place forms the horizontal foundation for the panonomic model, which is plotted against a transcendental understanding of time as the vertical. The vision for the model sees a dynamic 'whole spectrum' of place at its base, generating momentum through individual and collective contribution, to move in an 'upward spiral' motion toward the shared mission of time. In the model, time is conceived as transcendental, representing both our shared mission and our perpetual movement toward a 'Future Now'. Embedding this motility and dynamism within the panonomic framework means both that it reflects and embodies the dynamism of life, and that it is resistant to stasis. This in turn protects the model from the related threat of becoming no longer fit-for-purpose against a rapidly changing context.

Arguably, orthodox understandings of the economy have been subject to just this stasis and discord with the current—and future—contexts.

Panonomics proposes place as time as axes in a framework for a system of measurement which offers both complexity and simplicity. Complexity, through its horizontal axis of place, incorporating measures designed to draw out individual and collective experience of place, and simplicity, through its vertical axis, offering an opportunity to assess progress through the well-established and universally recognisable metrics of time. This system can be adopted at any scale, and so can be used both to measure the dynamics and progress of individual places, and their contribution to regional, national and global goals. In connecting the individual to the global, panonomics presents a fitting measurement system for the current and future dynamics of the 4.0 innovation age, and its characteristic as a deeply interconnected ecosystem (Scharmer 2016).

5.6 Summary: People Power

Panonomics is a people-powered and place-driven model, which offers a simple and unequivocal answer to the RSA's question about placemaking—'In the act of placemaking, who or what is doing the making? Who should be?' (RSA 2014).

The answer is the people and communities of the place.

References

Civil Exchange (2015) Whose Society? The Final Big Society Audit. London: Civil Exchange.

Gehl, J (1971) Life Between Buildings. Island Press.

Granovetter, M (1985) 'Economic Action and Social Structure, the Problem of Embeddedness', American Journal of Sociology Volume 91, Issue 3. Chicago: University of Chicago Press.

Pritchard, S (2017) Artwashing: Social Capital and Anti-Gentrification Activism. Accessed 13 December 2020.

RSA (2014) A Place for Heritage. London: The Royal Society of Arts and the Heritage Lottery Fund.

RSA (2017) Heritage, Identity and Place. London: The Royal Society of Arts and the Heritage Lottery Fund.

Rushton, E (2020) Squatting the Economy: Power to Change. Accessed 13 December 2020.

Scharmer, CO (2016) Theory U: Leading from the Future as It Emerges. Oakland: Berrett-Koehler Publishers

CHAPTER 6

Acting Now: 'The When'

Abstract The COVID-19 pandemic has brought additional urgency, impetus and imperative to the search for a new and fit-for-purpose organisational paradigm. At the same time as underlining our individual and collective vulnerability to crisis, the pandemic and lockdowns have also highlighted a latent human potential which, if maximised, could be the key to our future progress, resilience and achieving shared goals. The panonomic model has emerged from an exploration of the place/innovation nexus and, as such, this chapter sets our four recommendations for policymaking in support of place-driven innovation. It also sets out ten key actions which could—both individually and cumulatively—support and progress our transition to the panonomic model and journey through the 4.0 age. Some of the recommendations are simple, and some are more complex. No doubt, there will be challenge. But the key message of the chapter is a call to action. If not now, when?

Keywords Reset · Redistribute · Action · Transition · Progress · Purpose · Panonomics

C. Devaney, *Panonomics*,
https://doi.org/10.1007/978-3-030-87509-1_6

6.1 Introduction: A Moment in Time

In an era marked by polarisation, conflict and competition, *time* offers us a universal, accessible and fundamental shared goal. In the face of global, catastrophic crises which threaten our time together, our survival as a species and the sustainability of our planet, our principal concern and shared mission from this point forward should be the accumulation of more time.

The numerous limitations of our current economic model, which is based on a continued preoccupation with growth and productivity, resulting in widespread inequalities in every scale and all aspects of life, and in the accumulation of wealth for some and debt for others, have been roundly exposed by the COVID-19 pandemic and its devastating and disproportionate impacts. Work around new economic models, including explorations of alternatives to GDP as our accepted measure of economic progress, has been foregrounded as we seek a way through and beyond. The inability of the system to respond to the challenges of the pandemic with anywhere near the efficiency, agility or speed required has put us on high alert, raising deep concerns about our unpreparedness to face current and future challenges related to climate collapse. Further, the pandemic has initiated a deep and urgent questioning of our role in our own downfall as we continue to extract vital and limited resources from the planet, and as we continue extraction from human beings through exploitation and abuse, debt and rentierism, neglect and dereliction of care.

In the UK, the vast majority of our institutions and organisational structures are set up in support of continued polarisation and extraction or, at best, a 'Third Way' centrism and 'liberal guilt'. This is true of our political and governance institutions, our education system, the charity model, our media and the three acknowledged sectors of business—all mirroring the same model of public, private and somewhere in between. As we move toward a much more fluid and aware social zeitgeist, including in societal attitudes to gender and sexuality, these polarisations and half-way compromise no longer fit with our social norms or needs. 'A Fourth Way' presents a holistic model, founded on the principle of being neither left nor right nor in between, but an overarching and all-encompassing space. It envisages a reset and repurposing of the structures and systems that our holding us back, to be more attuned to and to service our needs, collective progress, survival and shared purpose.

Panonomics builds on 'A Fourth Way' as a framework to propose a new organisational model. The panonomic model, reflecting the etymology of its prefix, is a holistic and all-encompassing ecosystem, designed in support of collective investment and contribution toward a collective mission of making time.

Realising this vision will require a wholesale redesign and restructure of the mechanisms, institutions and organisations created in support of the currently dominant economic model, its inherent inequalities and focus on the free market, competition and perpetual (fiscal) growth. The structures in question are strong, powerful and prolific. Restructure presents a gargantuan task and a just and fair transition which would require a public mandate, no doubt in the face of a huge misinformation campaign which, as Alastair Parvin puts it 'would make Brexit look like a picnic' (Parvin 2020). Nevertheless, change of this scale has been achieved before and must be achieve it again if we are committed to the survival of our planet and our species. In his considered piece on the necessary reforms in land and property rights, Parvin compares the scale of change required to the abolition of slavery (Parvin 2020).

In the aftermath of the pandemic, The World Bank estimates that an additional 150 million people across the world will be living in extreme poverty by the end of 2021, taking the overall total to some 729 million (World Bank 2020).

Once again, our basic human morality demands change. The time to act is now.

6.2 Four Implications for Place/Innovation Policy

David Harvey describes globalisation as a 'downward spiral' and 'the annihilation of space over time' (Harvey 2017). Globalisation, which has overseen the stealth privatisation and associated attrition of public space (in both the physical and virtual realms), and in which space is commodified, commercialised, bought and sold, sits at the heart of the capitalist system. The resulting sustainability challenge which at its root cause has seen the human species colonise and strip the planet's spaces and natural resources to the point of ecosystem collapse (see Raworth 2017; Krznaric 2020), demands a new economic framing in which human and planetary survival is prioritised. Rather than promoting degrowth, a concept based on the protection of increasingly limited spatial resources, panonomics proposes an organisational system which is reframed to focus on time rather than space. In the panonomic model, time is prioritised as the primary and shared 'grand challenge' and global mission, building on Mazzucato's 'mission-oriented' model (Mazzucato 2017, 2021).

This reframing toward time has broad-reaching implications for policymaking and four key implications for place-related innovation policy.

Firstly, panonomics proposes a comprehensive and all-encompassing understanding of place as the basis for a place-driven organisational model. Applied to innovation, this asserts place-driven as an optimal approach (as opposed to the precedents of place-blind, place-based and place-grounded approaches). Panonomics envisages this place-driven expression of innovation as embracing 'the whole of life' (Williams 1958) of a place and the full extent of its human skills, technological capacity, tacit knowledge and lived experience. Policy in support of this open, expansive and place-driven model might come in the form of facilitating free access to open-source research and knowledge, cross-place networks and enhanced digital infrastructure.

Secondly, panonomics presupposes and requires collaboration, over competition. In regard to place strategies, which in many cases attempt to set out the relative strengths of a place as 'competitive advantage' over other places, this requires a reframing instead to support collaboration, bringing forward the unique contribution each place can make toward the shared mission. Innovation policies in which the concept of place is integral, including the European Commission's flagship approach of Smart Specialisation, are similarly predicated on 'competitive advantage' and will need to be reframed toward the 'competitive advantage' of the whole, supporting and fostering the shared application of innovation capacity toward shared, global challenges. In this new and inherently generative model, the extractive concept of 'productivity' is reframed as contribution.

Thirdly, there is a need to underscore place-driven innovation policies as strategies for diversification, rather than specialisation. Hassink and Gong (2019) refer to the concept of Smart Specialisation as 'confusing and conceptually chaotic', leading to misinterpretation and a limiting, rather than diversifying, effect. The panonomic model proposes that the route to diversification, to a more open and dynamic entrepreneurial discovery process, and to addressing the gaps and challenges which exist around marginalisation of individuals and communities (particularly on the basis of racial and ethnic marginalisation, but also apparent in terms of sex, gender and financial status), is through embedding innovation policy in the deep cultural heritage of each place, which in turn acts as the concrete foundation in Granovetter's 'concrete and ongoing social relations' (Granovetter 1985).

Finally, both place and innovation policies must seek to transcend the delineated time boundaries of the policy cycle. The 'short term risk-taking', for example, which is identified by Foray (2015) as a design principle for Smart Specialisation is at odds with what Krznaric calls the 'pathological short-termism' of our current political cycles and the 'short-term consumerist mores and growth-fixated economic model' (Krznaric 2020). Krznaric calls instead for a 'deep time humility' and 'promoting greater intergenerational justice, guided by the transcendent goal of creating a world in which the needs of future generations can be met with the resources on our finite planet', adding that 'one-planet thriving' should be a major goal of anyone aspiring to become a good ancestor. If people just don't care, we're doomed' (Krznaric 2020). Krznaric foregrounds both the importance of heritage and the importance of care. For too long, innovation policy has been allowed to operate at risk, with a care-free 'regenerative shedding' (Foray 2015) and scant regard for 'unintended negative consequences' (Rissola et al. 2017).

Panonomics challenges policy to care.

6.3 Making It Happen: Actions for the Now

While 'The Great Pause' (Janoo and Bone-Dodds 2020) offered opportunity to reflect, the pressing and dual imperatives of the pandemic and climate collapse mean that 'The Great Reset' (World Economic Forum 2020) must happen at scale and pace. The author makes the following ten recommendations for action. Some of these recommendations will require more investment of effort than others but should be actioned at the earliest opportunity. We must act like our 'Future Now' depends on it.

6.3.1 Embrace the Panonomic Paradigm

The panonomic paradigm is a holistic and all-encompassing systemic framework capable of both meeting the ongoing challenges of the COVID-19 pandemic, of promoting justice and equality and of maximising individual and collective contribution to sustainability goals. It is time to reject the economics of capital as no longer fit-for-purpose.

6.3.2 *Ditch GDP*

Extensive research and analysis around the limitations of GDP exists along with multiple proposals suggesting alternative dashboard and indexed indicators (see Hoekstra et al. 2020). Several countries, principally New Zealand, but also Iceland and Scotland, have initiated programmes which seek to measure progress in terms of wellbeing, but—to date—only as an addition to GDP measures. Progressing past the current stage of new and emerging proposals stuck as secondary systems of measurement demands that one or more countries have the courage to call time on GDP as an outdated, over-complicated and morally compromised measure of non-progress.

6.3.3 *Measure Progress*

Related to ridding ourselves of GDP, the structural mechanisms and organisations dedicated to measuring productivity, capital growth and competitive performance can be easily refocussed toward measuring experience and shared progress toward time and sustainability goals. Structures for measurement can be place-driven, feeding upwards from the grassroots of place through local, regional, national and global systems.

6.3.4 *Redistribute*

Panonomics starts from a platform of socialised wealth, using the word to capture the full richness of human and ecological capacity, wellbeing, knowledge and life. Achieving this foundational platform from here will require a large-scale and difficult, but not impossible, redistribution of wealth, whether that is 'short and sharp' or a process over time.

The first step in redistribution will be to acquire a transparent understanding of the current distribution of (comprehensive) wealth, a task which might be undertaken by those newly restructured organisations previously busied with the measuring of growth and GDP.

Globally, redistribution of land wealth must include reparations.

On a smaller scale, redistribution might build on the success of 'Community Wealth Building' and start with agreement from 'Anchor Institutions' (and other landowners and developers) to incorporate a covenant toward socialised ownership of land, knowledge and other assets. These could also be a feature of any state supported development deals as a new form of 'asset lock'. This should be accompanied by a restructuring of public budgets so that, for example, housing becomes part of public utility infrastructure and which might include, again as an example, ringfencing budget to provide free meals for schoolchildren (perhaps redeploying some of the £16.5bn announced in November 2020 as ringfenced for UK defence).

6.3.5 *Growth as Purpose and Progress*

In the reset, growth should be reframed as shared purpose and progress toward collective goals. The organisations set up to pursue endless capital growth can be refocussed on our collective, broad-scope wealth and human and planetary sustainability. Support should be available, on the same scale as business growth advice is currently, for people and organisations seeking to contribute to sustainability goals. For too many years, social enterprises have been ill-served by 'business growth' support and obliged to report as 'not for profit'. As a transitional measure and in order to highlight areas needing support to contribute toward sustainability goals, we might instigate the reverse and request that businesses who do not meet sustainability criteria report as 'not for purpose'.

6.3.6 *Positive Governance*

As is the case with GDP and measures of productivity, we have also outgrown the institutions of governance. A prime example can be observed in the polarised, theatrical politics played out in the UK's Houses of Parliament, from the filibustering on the benches and the ostentatious displays of 'The Queen's Speech', to the analogue practices of MPs voting on foot and its 'raffle ticket' system for inclusion in Prime Minister's Questions. There are opportunities at all levels to utilise the full capacity of our technological capability as the basis for increased participation and an improved democracy. Partisan politics is also well past its time. 'A Fourth Way' envisages a holistic, spectrum politics which rejects the polarities of partisanship and promotes positive governances toward shared goals. Our transition to a 'Future Now' must include a democratic reset of our institutions of governance.

6.3.7 *The State as a Social Movement*

The pandemic has highlighted the role of voluntary organisations and the third sector in propping up a significantly reduced (and slow to respond) state. It is an unacceptable and unpalatable situation, already played out by Cameron's 'Big Society', to expect hard-pressed charities to 'fill in' for a lack of state provision while cuts continue to funding streams and front-line services. That said, we have also seen how deep local connections have meant that these organisations are better placed to serve local communities, as well as being more agile than the current state and quicker to respond and innovate to changing needs. Given this direction of travel, our transition might be better served in formally devolving state funds for provision of services to the third and 'social sector', embracing new and emerging social movements within and as part of the state (and supported by its monies). Creating a new and overarching 'fourth sector', the state itself will in effect be realised as a new social movement.

6.3.8 *Transform Finance*

Current funding and financing structures are unable to support our transformational transition. Financial markets prefer stability and status-quo which, as Hofstetter (2020) observes is incompatible with the complexities and turbulence of transformation (aligned with the difficulties in rationalising the implied embeddedness of place with the inherent dynamism of innovation). Hofstetter's vision for what he calls 'Transformation Capital' 'embraces the state as a confident and bold entrepreneur', proposing targeted investment in 'Sensitive Intervention Points' (SIPs), small investments catalysing big change, and asserting a systemic directionality by actively shaping markets in pursuit of that direction. The panonomic model offers the perfect systemic platform for this approach, proposing time as the shared mission and systemic directionality, and a burgeoning social movement as the new state. New models of banking which offer a more compatible route for transitional funds should be pursued, including opportunities for place-driven investment banks (local, regional, national and global).

6.3.9 *Onward and Upward*

Panonomics proposes a directionality for growth as purpose and progress, conceptualised as an 'upward spiral' flow. This is not a call for more devolution, which distributes power outward and downward from a central point, but more in the vein of a wholesale, constitutional, federal reform—from the ground up. It is distinct, too from the direction of 'recycled wealth' programmes, where wealth is gathered and redirected back downward toward the point of origin (as in the practice of 'Community Wealth Building'). This is a place-driven model, with citizens and communities in the driving seat.

6.3.10 *Mission: Time*

'Mission creep' is a well-known phenomenon in military and organisational strategy, which denotes a gradual broadening of objectives to the extent that the original purpose of the mission is forgotten or neglected. It comes with a cautionary tone as its use implies the danger of failure due to losing sight of the intended goal. Arguably, we have been suffering from 'mission creep' as a human race, particularly—but not exclusively—from an economic perspective. We need to embrace time as our shared mission, prioritising the survival of our species and our planet.

6.4 Summary: If Not Now, When?

Historically, pandemics have forced humans to break with the past and imagine their world anew. This one is no different. It is a portal, a gateway between one world and the next. We can choose to walk through it, dragging the carcasses of our prejudice and hatred, our avarice, our data banks and dead ideas, our dead rivers and smoky skies behind us. Or we can walk through lightly, with little luggage, ready to imagine another world. And ready to fight for it.

—Arundhati Roy (2020)

The COVID-19 pandemic and its lockdowns have, to some extent, enabled us to explore and test out new models of living and being in real time. Despite its many and vast challenges, this year has evidenced the power of community and cooperation and given us a small glimpse into what an economy might look like decoupled from the endless demands of growth and productivity. This has been particularly true of the world of work, with office life and the daily commute increasingly replaced by home working and online collaborative platforms (although even these have their downsides and limitations).

This new approach to working has reignited calls for Universal Basic Income and Universal Basic Services, alongside proposals for a shorter working week (should a return to the office be on the cards). Potentially freed from the tyranny of having to work to secure food or shelter, the concept of liberated time holds all sorts of creative possibility. Work might no longer be regarded as 'earning a living', with a living and the right to it assured. Staying in a lifetime job to pay a lifetime mortgage could be a thing of the past.

Assertion of a holistic model brings huge implications for our understanding of skills, which have previously been viewed primarily in service of the economy, and lessons too for our still-Victorian education system and its preparation for conforming to a life of work—sitting in rows, 'good' behaviour and moving around to the bell. Reform will also be needed in how our model of charity operates (also Victorian), through which billions have been donated to combat various issues and inequalities and which doubtless has generated much-needed emergency and short-term solutions, but which over years of continued investment has shown little long-term success. In 2020, we should not need footballers to need to advocate for feeding our children.

The panonomic model proposes a vision of holistic prosperity, rather than the dominance of links to productivity at a theory level, and to (monetary) wealth in practice, a wealth accumulated at the expense of others. Our shared prosperity—our collective wealth—is presented in the panonomic model as our starting point and foundation for onward progress, driven not by competition, but by collaboration, and not in support of extraction, but of individual and collective contribution.

A major pinch-point of transitioning to a new model on these terms will be land ownership, and property which, one suspects, will be a particularly hard sell to land and property owners. Again, the pandemic has allowed us to test out some waters. Creating even temporary solutions to crises previously thought of as beyond solution have inspired hope in what we can achieve. In a brave new world, we can imagine that housing which has been both commodified and limited to create a false market demand might be enshrined as a human right and in plentiful supply. Community trust covenants can—fairly easily—be built into all development deals (or, to start, all deals supported by state funding). The Community

Wealth Building movement might continue to progress its work with 'Anchor Institutions' such as universities, who might feasibly covenant their land to local communities and grant open access to their most valuable resource—knowledge. In this new era of collective ownership, hospitals could finally be freed from crippling PFI agreements (another legacy of 'The Third Way').

In a time-focussed economy, provision of care—of time—and therefore our ultimate investment, will be prioritised and valued as our key industry. Development projects need no longer be framed in terms of spend—'a £14bn creative industry hub'—but in terms of what they will generate for us, in time. It will be enough to express volunteering hours in hours, without ascribing a value to the individual's time to convert into pounds. So-called social value will not need to be expressed as a monetary 'return on investment'. Road safety projects can be celebrated by the number of lives saved, without the need for additional cost–benefit analysis. All of this is possible and achievable.

Panonomics proposes that our shared, and urgent, mission is the collective accumulation of time. There is nothing to be gained by wasting it.

References

Foray, D (2015) Smart Specialisation: Opportunities and Challenges for Regional Innovation Policy. London: Routledge.

Granovetter, M (1985) 'Economic Action and Social Structure, the Problem of Embeddedness', American Journal of Sociology Volume 91, Issue 3. Chicago: University of Chicago Press.

Harvey, D (2017) Marx, Capital and the Madness of Economic Reason. London: Profile.

Hassink, R, and Gong, H (2019) Six Critical Questions About Smart Specialization. Taylor & Francis.

Hoekstra, R et al (2020) 'Measuring the Wellbeing Economy: How to Go Beyond-GDP'. Wellbeing Economy Alliance.

Hofstetter, D (2020) https://medium.com/transformation-capital/transformation-capital-systemic-investing-for-sustainability-693cb1190da. Accessed 14 December 2020.

Janoo, A, and Bone-Dodds, G (2020) The Great Pause. Open Democracy: The Great Pause|openDemocracy.

Krznaric, R (2020) The Good Ancestor. London: Penguin.

Mazzucato, M (2017) The Entrepreneurial State. London: Penguin.

Mazzucato, M (2021) Mission Economy. London: Penguin.
Parvin, A (2020) https://alastairparvin.medium.com/a-new-land-contract-684c3ba1f1b3. Accessed 14 December 2020.
Raworth, K (2017) Doughnut Economics. London: Random.
Rissola, G, Hervás, F, Slavcheva, M, and Jonkers, K (2017) Place-Based Innovation Ecosystems: Espoo Innovation Garden and Aalto University (Finland). Luxembourg: Publications Office of the European Union.
Roy, A (2020) The Pandemic Is a Portal. https://www.ft.com/content/10d8f5e8-74eb-11ea-95fe-fcd274e920ca. Financial Times, 3 April 2020. Accessed 4 July 2021.
Williams, R (1958) Culture Is Ordinary. Grantmakers in the Arts (GIA) https://www.giarts.org/article/culture-ordinary. Accessed 4 July 2021.
World Bank (2020) Poverty Overview (worldbank.org). Accessed 4 July 2021.
World Economic Forum (2020) The Great Reset. Accessed 4 July 2021.

CHAPTER 7

Panonomics: A 4.0 System to Save Us from Ourselves

Abstract This chapter summarises the thinking behind panonomics and its conceptual framework, characterised as 'A Fourth Way'. It includes an exploration of 'A Fourth Way' principles and a tabular summary of application of 'A Fourth Way' thinking to a range of concepts and constructs which have previously been established accepted as tripartite. Panonomics is based on an adoption of the holism proposed by 'A Fourth Way' as an organisational system. In concluding comments, the author sets out how the panonomic model can support our journey to and through the 4.0 innovation age and from the now to the next.

Keywords Place · Time · Innovation · Culture · Human · A Fourth Way · Panonomics

7.1 Introduction: Four: That's the Magic Number

Panonomics embraces the power of four as the basis for progression to the 4.0 age. Adoption of a fourth perspective rejects artificial binaries and polarities, and the consensus of the middle ground to instead envisage an all-encompassing whole; a fourth space. Application of this thinking to policy and practice as 'A Fourth Way' has the potential to elevate a whole

C. Devaney, *Panonomics*,
https://doi.org/10.1007/978-3-030-87509-1_7

range of concepts, constructs, structures and systems previously established and accepted as tripartite. Applying this thinking to the concepts of place and time reveals a deep and comprehensive understanding of both. This depth of understanding is applied in the proposed panonomic model, which plots these deep comprehensions as the horizontal and vertical axes of its core framework, and in doing so offers a model which is both simple and complex, dynamic and embedded, for the now and for the 'Future Now'.

7.2 'A Fourth Way': Conceptual Framework

Application of 'A Fourth Way' thinking elevates previously established binaries and tripartite frameworks within a fourth space, revealing a new taxonomy for place and, at the fourth level, the key characteristics of panonomics as a place-driven paradigm for the 4.0 innovation age.

These concepts and constructs, their manifest and inter-relationships within a fourth space are discussed in further detail in the subsequent sections and are summarised as a conceptual framework in Table 7.1.

7.2.1 A New Place Taxonomy

Moving beyond established binaries and tripartite structures to reach a conceptual fourth space reveals in turn a new taxonomy for place, adding logic and coherence to its currently inchoate definition and usage. The new taxonomy proposes an iterative flow toward a deeper understanding of place, which moves in succession through 'place-blind', 'place-based' and 'place-grounded' strategies to reach 'place-driven', as a key characteristic of 'A Fourth Way' and, by extension, of panonomics.

Each of the expressions of place is attached to an interrogative concept (the where, what, who and how) and mapped to a related construct (spatial, commercial, cultural, communal), sector profile (private, public/academic, social/3rd sector and grassroots), economic sequence (1.0, 2.0, 3.0, 4.0) and, building on the work of Otto Scharmer (2016), a related dominant economic characteristic (state-centric, free market, socio-economic, ecosystem).

Table 7.1 Panonomics—A 'Fourth Way' conceptual framework

SEQUENCE	INNOVATION SPACE	SECTOR	CONSTRUCT	PLACE	SHIFT	ECONOMY	INDUSTRY	INNOVATION POLICY	TIME	CONCEPT
1.0	Science Parks	Private	Spatial	Place-blind	Subject	State-centric	Primary/ Extraction	Science/ R&D	Historical	WHERE
2.0	Anchor Plus	Public/ Academic	Commercial	Place-based	Consumer	Free-Market	Secondary/ Manufacture	National Systems	Chronological	WHAT
3.0	Reimagined Urban Areas	Social/ 3rd	Cultural	Place-grounded	Citizen	Socio-Economic	Tertiary/ Services	Transformative Change	Inter-Temporal	WHO
4.0	Commons	Grassroots	Communal	Place-driven	Human	Ecosystem	Quaternary/ Contribution	Evolutionary	Transcendental	HOW
CONCEPT	WHERE	WHAT	WHO	HOW				WHY		

7.2.2 *The Place/Innovation Nexus in 4.0*

Each of these expressions of place and their related economic profiles (Scharmer 2016) is also attached to one of the three key typologies of innovation district, as identified by Katz and Wagner (2014). Sitting alongside a deeper understanding of place, these typologies reveal an increasingly dynamic expression of innovation, running sequentially as 'anchor plus' (mapped here to Economy 1.0 and place-blind approaches), 'urbanized science park' (mapped here to Economy 2.0 and place-based approaches) and 'reimagined urban areas' (mapped here to Economy 3.0 and place-grounded approaches).

Each innovation typology is also mapped to Schot and Steinmuller's 2018 propositions around policy frames for innovation. Schot and Steinmuller propose a post-war framing in science and R&D as 'Innovation 1.0', a focus on national innovation systems as 'Innovation 2.0' and an emerging focus on 'transformative change' and socio-technical ecosystems as 'Innovation 3.0' (Schot and Steinmuller 2018). 'A Fourth Way' proposes a fourth layer to this proposition as 'Innovation 4.0', bringing together the how (of place) and the why (of time) in its characterisation as an evolutionary innovation.

7.2.3 *A Culture Shift*

Arguably the dominant understandings of place as a fixed spatial/private ('the where') and socio-economic/commercial territory ('the what') have been extended to innovation, and specifically to innovation districts, with only superficial attention paid to social relations/cultural factors ('the who') and even less to the dynamics of those factors ('the how'). Introduction of a cultural construct at the 'third level' of the place taxonomy is pivotal in the shift from 'place-blind' and 'place-based' to unlocking 'place-grounded' and 'place-driven' approaches, each with increasing levels of depth in terms of 'embeddedness'. Opening up innovation strategies to the potential for embracing the full diversity, richness and cultural 'whole way of life' (Williams 1958) of a place, its social relations and cultural heritage, offers a route through which the territorial limitations and perceived (and real) boundaries of innovation can be transcended, allowing a fuller exploration and expression of the 'place-driven' model as 'the how' of innovation 4.0.

7.2.4 A Human Shift

This shift toward cultural authenticity sits alongside a discernible shift toward 'community', community leadership and agency, which is evident too in several emerging economic development models such as 'Community Wealth Building' (Guinan et al. 2020), 'Doughnut Economics' (Raworth 2017) and mission-oriented approaches (Mazzucato 2017, 2021), all of which assert a 'ground-up' directionality and an enhanced role for individuals and grassroots communities. The New Citizenship Project (NCP) highlights this shift toward community activism in what they call the 'Citizen Shift' (NCP 2015), a three-stage evolutionary model which asserts a shift in individual and collective conscious from ***subjects*** to ***consumers*** to ***citizens***. Real-life examples of this shift include The Black Lives Matter (BLM) movement, the #metoo movement and school strikes in protest of climate change (inspired by Greta Thunberg), as well as the expressions of collectivism and care that have emerged during the COVID-19 pandemic.

When applied to the new place taxonomy, an additional expression is proposed as a 'fourth layer' to NCP (2015)'s subject—consumer—citizen model, asserting a distinctly ***human*** approach as the relational characteristic of 4.0 and 'A Fourth Way'. This human-centric approach lies at the heart of a new paradigm and is central to the way in which innovation is manifest in the 4.0 age—'the how'.

7.2.5 Anchor-Y in the UK

Anchor institutions are central to Katz and Wagner's 'anchor plus' typology of innovation district and to the emerging practice of 'Community Wealth Building' (Guinan et al. 2020). The Centre for Local Economic Strategies (CLES), a chief proponent of the Community Wealth Building movement in the UK, includes local authorities, NHS trusts, universities, trade unions, large local businesses and housing associations in its given examples of anchor institutions, organisations which 'have an important presence in a place, usually through a combination of being largescale employers, the largest purchasers of goods and services in the locality, controlling large areas of land and/or having relatively fixed assets and/or that are tied to a particular place by their mission, histories, physical assets and local relationships' (CLES 2017).

Katz and Wagner conceive of the 'anchor plus' model of innovation as one in which 'large scale mixed-use development is centered around major anchor institutions and a rich base of related firms, entrepreneurs and spin-off companies involved in the commercialization of innovation' (Katz and Wagner 2014). The explicit relationship between anchor institutions and commercialisation noted by Katz and Wagner is reflected too in the conceptual framework for 'A Fourth Way'. While potentially contentious this assertion represents an important paradigm shift in the manifest of commercial activity (traditionally positioned firmly in the 'private sector' orbit) and the increasingly commercial behaviours of both public sector and academic anchors (traditionally regarded as non-commercial extensions of the state).

7.2.6 *Place and Time: 'The How' and 'The Why'*

The panonomic model plots place against time, utilising 'A Fourth Way' conceptual framework to reveal and apply a deep and comprehensive understanding of the formerly inchoate concept of place, and the perpetual mystery of time. Applying the holism of a fourth space thinking, which in essence rejects polarity and the 'Third Way' compromise of the middle-ground, 'A Fourth Way' offers a new vision of a human-centred, grassroots and place-driven innovation ecosystem, which is capable of supporting our shared progress through the 4.0 innovation age.

Place, as a complex and dynamic network of multiple characteristics is presented as the key to how the panonomic model will work as an organisational model, and the accumulation of time, as a transcendental metric of progress, is presented as our shared goal and primary purpose—the why.

7.3 Panonomics: Summary and Final Comments

Panonomics is founded on principles of equality, fairness and justice and seeks abandonment of our current system's reliance on 'winners and losers'. We must restructure the institutions, organisations and outdated practices holding us back from progress. This includes, and from an economic analysis point of view, prioritises a rejection of GDP and its productivity measures. The dance with GDP has got to stop. We need to rescue 'the economy' from its hijack as referring only to finance when it is much broader than that. This will require, too, restructuring of the organisations established to support competition between places and our 'Stockholm syndrome' pursuit of growth at all costs, to instead measure and support our sustainability and survival. To some extent, the restructuring is happening already, with countries including New Zealand, Iceland and Scotland adopting wellbeing indicators within their economic measuring systems, but only alongside GDP. This has resulted in a plethora of ideas around 'sustainable growth', 'inclusive growth' and strategies which claim to be 'globally competitive and socially inclusive'. These collections of words are oxymoronic. We cannot have sustainability and growth, inclusion and growth or competition and inclusion. The only thing we can grow sustainably, ad infinitum, is time.

More broadly, there is a job of work to be done in resetting our democratic systems and institutions of governance to be fit for purpose. Our experience in the UK has seen the state exposed by the pandemic as limited, lacking and inefficient, even inert, juxtaposed with an agile and responsive third, voluntary, community and civic space, which managed to adapt its focus and operations efficiently and effectively, working at depth and speed to meet immediate needs. Panonomics proposes a dynamic and innovative 'Fourth Sector' state, operating as a social movement, funded by new and responsive banking models such as socialised investment banks and public wealth funds, shaped to better support our transition and transformation and—critically—to ensure that we are better prepared for climate collapse, and the challenges to come.

The scale of this ambition might, to some, seem immature or unachievable. This is a standard argument for the status quo, generally put forward by those who benefit from the status quo. Rather, there is a particular naivety and some ignorance in blithely accepting the current, patriarchal system and particularly in a continued belief in aspects such as 'trickle down' when there is little evidence to support any such trickling. Arguably, it is a more mature approach to be open to possibilities and alternatives and to act in setting the course rather than being along for the ride. New ideas need to have a level of ambition to inspire progress. Translating new ideas into workable systems takes a collective effort. Every new system is seen as new-fangled or outrageous until it becomes normalised, and systems take time to bed in. My mother still refers to decimalisation as a state crime and, she suspects, a diversionary tactic for something even more sinister.

Sadly, in accepting the norms and parameters of our current system, led by capitalism and its neoliberal horsemen, we have accepted, or at least become ignorant to, its inherent unfairness and immorality so that horrors like poverty and destitution has been normalised. Just the word 'destitution' should fill us with fear and guilt and, yes, outrage. To think that millions of people the world over, and hundreds of thousands in the UK are destitute, that they cannot afford to eat or to keep warm. Perhaps it is the scale that waters it down for us. We are unable to conceive of something so horrific. But we can see destitution every day, in our cities and on our streets. Eight thousand people in Greater Manchester are homeless, and eighty thousand more waiting on the list for social housing (BBC News 2020). In a 2020 report, the Joseph Rowntree Foundation reveals that the majority of people have reached the point of destitution through debt, mainly to local authorities, the state (specifically the Department of Work and Pensions) and utility companies (JRF 2020). People are being made destitute because they owe money to the state, and further to the DWP whose purpose in terms of welfare provision is to support those people with a safety net in lieu of work, in order to avoid the very poverty and destitution to which they are currently condemning them. It is worth noting too that the other primary sources of debt are council tax and utility companies. The logistics of having a home is making people homeless. United Utilities features in the 'Top 50' landowners in the country (ABC Finance 2020).

Debt relief (and cancellation) and reparations must be part of the reset and we must explore and progress socialised models of land ownership. We cannot approach either established institutions or authorities of any scale as benign extensions of the citizenry. Local authority is not synonymous with community. Many universities act more like private sector corporates, commercialising knowledge and innovation, charging extraordinary tuition fees and holding vast amounts of land. A number of charities too are huge landowners. An extreme example here can be found in Cleveland, US where a community charity has recently been announced as a partner in Cleveland's developing 'innovation district'. That charity, the Cleveland Foundation, has over $2.5bn in assets. Economy does not mean money; charity does not mean poor and green does not mean good. Like tech before it, green infrastructure is just as susceptible to takeover and monopolisation. Trees are making their way into investment portfolios. It is not enough to paint capitalism green and expect it to change.

During the pandemic, 15,000 rough sleepers in the UK were accommodated in vacant hotel rooms, alleviating and in some places eradicating a humanitarian crisis which we had previously been told was insurmountable. Although it is ambitious for our now and for our future, nothing set out in this book is unachievable. We set up these structures, and we can set up new ones. We designed this economy, and we can design the next. As the inequalities and negative, some devastating, impacts of the current system grow more pronounced, the 'can' in this sentence is becoming a 'must'. We must design the next.

Contemporary society is not only marked by polarisation, but also by powerful civic movements, people and communities coming together to demand justice and enact change. It will take all of our collective talents, skills, empathy, creativity and contribution to transition into the next, panonomic system.

Panonomics offers a timely and universal response to the current and universal challenges of the pandemic. It presents a 'catch all' framework in which the burgeoning new economic movement can unify and to mobilise. Mair (2020) proposes that a renewed focus on the question of what economies produce, and who they produce it for, can create a space in which connections between movements can be built. Panonomics presents a simple and effective response to that call, both in creating a horizontal space in which movements can happily coexist, but also in directing that holistic wealth of movement and passion and activism toward a shared economic purpose, produce and collective mission, of making time. At a time when we are feeling uncomfortable in our economic skin, panonomics offers an ergonomic and human-centred concept which will allow us not only to look after our own house, but to look after everyone's houses.

Panonomics can take us from the now to the next.

References

ABC Finance (2020) The UK's Largest Landowners Revealed|ABC Finance Ltd. Accessed 4 July 2021.

BBC News (2020) https://www.bbc.co.uk/news/uk-england-manchester-55208787. Accessed 14 December 2020.

CLES (2017) What Is an Anchor Institution? https://cles.org.uk/what-is-community-wealth-building/what-is-an-anchor-institution/. Accessed 4 July 2021.

Guinan, J, Mcinroy, N, Liebowitz, J, and McKinley, S (2020) Owning the Future: After Covid-19, A New Era of Community Wealth Building. Manchester: CLES.

Joseph Rowntree Foundation. (2020). https://www.jrf.org.uk/report/destitution-uk-2020. Accessed 14 December 2020.

Katz, B, and Wagner, J (2014). The Rise of Innovation Districts: A New Geography of Innovation in America. Washington: Brookings.

Mair, S (2020) Neoliberal Economics, Planetary Health, and the COVID-19 Pandemic: A Marxist Ecofeminist Analysis. https://www.thelancet.com/journals/lanplh/article/PIIS2542-5196(20)30252-7/fulltext. Elsevier Open Access. Accessed 14 December 2020.

New Citizenship Project (2015) This Is the Citizen Shift. https://newcitizenshipproject.wordpress.com/2015/10/28/this-is-the-citizen-shift/. Accessed 4 July 2021.

Raworth, K (2017) Doughnut Economics. London: Random.

Scharmer, CO (2016) Theory U: Leading from the Future as it Emerges. Oakland: Berrett-Koehler Publishers.

Schot, Johan, and Steinmueller, W. Edward (2018) Three Frames for Innovation Policy: R&D, Systems of Innovation and Transformative Change. Elsevier.

Wagner, J (2020) How Cleveland's Innovation District is Advancing Equity Through a New Kind of Anchor Institution. Washington: Brookings.

Williams, R (1958) Culture Is Ordinary. Grantmakers in the Arts (GIA). https://www.giarts.org/article/culture-ordinary. Accessed 4 July 2021.

Glossary

Community A collective of individuals sharing a common location, attitude, belief or interest.

Culture The ideas, customs, behaviours, arts, skills, intellectual product, knowledge, belief, laws, customs and way of life of a community or collective.

Cultural Heritage Inherited traditions (relationships, practices, rituals, events, knowledge and skills) and built structures (buildings, monuments and sites) that are acknowledged as having importance and/or are valued by, to and for a community.

Embeddedness The quality or state of being deeply linked, inter-related and/or interdependent to or within a sphere of activity, environment, context, structure, institution, organisation, logic or rules.

Entrepreneurial Discovery A process in which actors scan for opportunities to produce and use innovation and to implement innovation processes.

Innovation The act or process of implementing a new method or idea.

Innovation Districts Defined and bounded geographic areas within an urban economy in which there is a marked concentration of firms who identify as producing and/or using innovation and innovation processes.

Place A geographical location connected to individual or collective emotional and/or sentimental meaning.

C. Devaney, *Panonomics*,
https://doi.org/10.1007/978-3-030-87509-1

Policymaking The process of producing a set of rules, laws, ideas or plans that is used as a basis for making political, economic, planning and investment decisions.

Smart Specialisation A policy framework designed to support regional areas to identify, enhance and scale potential areas of competitive advantage through research and development.

Space A boundless extent formed of height, width and depth.

Sustainability The ability to be maintained at a certain level, commonly applied in current usage to the capacity for the planetary biosphere and human civilisation to co-exist.

Time An ongoing, measured or relational period in which actions, processes, events or occurrences exist or continue.

Index

C. Devaney, *Panonomics*,
https://doi.org/10.1007/978-3-030-87509-1

The manufacturer's authorised representative in the EU is Springer Nature Customer Service Centre GmbH, Europaplatz 3, 69115 Heidelberg, Germany. If you have any concerns regarding our products, please contact ProductSafety@springernature.com

Printed and bound by CPI Group (UK) Ltd, Croydon, CR0 4YY

30/09/2026

02225472-0002